MW01107657

Preparing the Bride

Who Is Jesus Returning For?

James A. Cousineau

WestBow Press books may be ordered through booksellers or by contacting:

WestBow Press
A Division of Thomas Nelson
1663 Liberty Drive
Bloomington, IN 47403
www.westbowpress.com
1-(866) 928-1240

ISBN: 978-1-4497-0991-4 (sc)
ISBN: 978-1-4497-0993-8 (dj)
ISBN: 978-1-4497-0992-1 (e)

Library of Congress Control Number: 2010942203

Printed in the United States of America

WestBow Press rev. date: 02/08/2011

ACKNOWLEDGMENTS AND DEDICATION

I would like to thank those who have helped in preparing this manuscript: Whitney for your typing, Joanna for proof-reading and typing corrections and Elena for proof-reading.

I especially want to express my love and appreciation to my wife who was the driving force and encouragement needed to get this book published.

Finally and most important I want to thank and give praise to my Lord and Savior Jesus Christ who enabled me to write this book and to whom it is dedicated.

Contents

I. The Call to Commitment/God Desires, Deserves and Demands Wholehearted Love 1

1. The Second Coming: Who is Jesus Coming For? 2
2. Get and Keep Your Heart Right. 5
3. It All Comes Down To Love! 8
4. God Desires, Deserves and Demands our Wholehearted Love. 11
5. What Is True Love? 14
6. Love is More Than A Feeling!. 19
7. Call My People To Commitment 22

II. Characteristics of Commitment/God's standard of Love 25

8. A New Commandment 26
9. What Kind Of Bride Is Jesus Coming For? 28
10. God Gives Grace to the Humble 31
11. Developing the Heart of a Servant 34
12. Obedience and Commitment 37
13. No Greater Love. . . Sacrifice 40

III: Cultivating our Love for and Commitment to God 45

14. Do You Really Love Me? 46
15. You Have Left Your First Love!. 48
16. He Who is Forgiven Much, Loves Much!. 51
17. How Much Love Does The Lord Expect?. 54
18. Forgetting What Lies Behind 57
19. Put Away Your Idols. 61
20. Do Not Love the World or the Things of the World 65
21. Get Rid of the Last Days Lovers 69
22. It is Time to Wake Up!. 72
23. Be Filled with the Fullness of God 76
24. Seek the Lord With All Your Heart 80
25. Seek the Lord Early, Everywhere and Often (Psalm 63) 84
26. Worship is the Key. 89

27. Rejoice in the Lord Always! 94
28. Trust in the Lord With all your Heart 98
29. Communication is the key: Know and Do the Word 104
30. My Sheep Hear My Voice and Follow Me 109
31. Encourage One Another All the More... 113
32. The Great Commission 118
33. Abide in the Vine! 122
34. Led by the Spirit of God 126
35. The Fear of the Lord 131
36. What Manner of Persons Ought We to Be?!! 135

I.

The Call to Commitment/God Desires, Deserves and Demands Wholehearted Love

1

The Second Coming: Who is Jesus Coming For?

These days there is much talk about the end times, Bible prophecy, and the second coming of Christ. Believers and non-believers alike are recognizing the signs of the times and wondering if this could be the Last Days that are spoken of in some way by most of the major religions. Hollywood has fueled and capitalized on this concern by producing many films with an apocalyptic theme. Radio and TV talk show hosts have brought on numerous guests to discuss this hot topic. Even on a national news broadcast I heard one commentator state that in a poll nearly 70% of Americans believe we are living in the last days and that it could even happen in the next few years.

This book is not intended to debate whether or not this event will actually happen. As a follower of Jesus Christ and one who has diligently read and studied the word of God for many years, I know that the second coming of Christ is a given. In John 14:2-3, Jesus says that He is preparing a place for His disciples and promises to come again to receive them and take them to be with Him. Also in Acts 1:9-10, when Jesus was taken up to heaven after His resurrection and brief appearance to His disciples, an angel declares that this same Jesus will return in like manner. There are many other verses in scripture that also point to the certainty of this event and even describe some of the events preceding His coming.

The many Bible prophecies and end time descriptions are a matter of intense study and debate today as people seek to discover the actual timing of these events. There are numerous excellent books and teachings on prophecy by people more scholarly than I, and I encourage you to prayerfully read or listen to some of these...

Since Jesus Himself stated that no on would know the hour or the day, many have concluded, "Then why should we think and worry about it?" However, He went on to warn His disciples that His coming would be sudden and unexpected for those who were not prepared, just "like a thief in the night." Therefore, He commanded them (and us today) to watch, pray and be ready!

During the time of the first advent, in spite of the many prophecies that were fulfilled exactly as they had been foretold and the miracles which were meant to confirm His identity, many would reject Him. Because their hearts were not prepared, they were blind to the true nature of His Kingdom and they did not know the time of their visitation or the things that would bring true inner peace and well being. This would lead to their eventual judgment and destruction.

Lk. 19:42-44

God knew how important it was for His people to recognize and receive His Son so He sent John before Him in order to prepare them. John was described as a forerunner of the Messiah who was to make ready a people prepared for the Lord. He declared himself to be a voice crying in the wilderness, "Prepare the way of the Lord. Make His paths straight." The message he preached of repentance and surrender made it clear that the preparation required was a matter of the heart. There were many religious people of the day whose outward appearance and actions seemed to indicate they certainly were the ones who would be chosen. They were proud of their good work and sure that God would be equally impressed. However, they were rebuked by both John and Jesus as being a "brood of vipers" and "whitewashed tombs", looking good on the outside but dead inside. Further, Jesus said they were people who honored Him with their lips but their hearts were far from Him.

Lk. 1:17

Before His return Jesus promised that there also would be people who would operate in this same manner as John, in the spirit and power of Elijah, to prepare His people. Like John, they will desire only to attend the bridegroom and help prepare the bride for the great marriage of the Lamb, which will only happen when the bride has made herself ready. So the

Rev. 19:7
22:17
22:20

friend of the bridegroom with the help of the Holy Spirit will continue to make things ready for His coming. At the right time the Spirit and the bride will say, "Come!" Jesus will say, "I am coming quickly." To which His prepared bride will exclaim, "Amen, Even so, come, Lord Jesus!"

When Jesus returns, He will be coming in His full glory as the King of Kings and Lord of lords, unlike His first coming when he emptied Himself and became of no reputation taking the form of a baby. The day of the Lord is declared to be a Great and Terrible Day for that reason. Truly it will be a glorious day for those whose hearts are right and ready, but it will be judgment for those who, for whatever reason, have not made the necessary preparations.

So, the important question in these exciting days is not when is He coming, but who is He coming for and will I be among those He receives to Himself? Since the Bible does say that many are called but few are chosen, what must I do to be among the chosen, those invited to the marriage supper of the Lamb? As we watch the signs of the times and see the day fast approaching, we need also to be praying for and listening to His instructions. "Lord, give us ears to hear what the Spirit is saying to the church in this crucial hour!" Then, if we are going to be among those who are prepared for His coming, we must be willing to quickly and completely obey Him in everything or risk being left behind (as the popular book and movie series portrays!) What a terrible thing to hear the door being locked, to know it's too late, and to hear, "Depart from me. I never knew you..."

I have asked the Lord to help me be one of the few who will be ready and chosen to be with Him forever. How can I keep from being one of the many on the path that leads to destruction, or one of the many who will be deceived and fall away in these difficult last days? There are many voices clamoring for our attention, and the church in America seems to be going in so many different directions that it can be very confusing and frustrating. How can I stay on the right path and keep from being discouraged, distracted and/or deceived away from God's intended purpose for my life and His church? If you have had some of these same questions and are also sensing the urgency of the hour, then keep reading. The answer the Lord gave me brought me back to His original call for me to ministry and is the subject of this book...

2

Get and Keep Your Heart Right

When God first brought me to Himself and demonstrated His love for me through His Son Jesus Christ, I was overwhelmed and determined to love, worship and serve Him the rest of my life. He especially gave me a heart for the church, and though I have always sought to lead people to Jesus, my deepest desire has been to see people grow up to maturity so that together we would come to the 'fullness of the measure of the stature of Christ'. My passion is that the church would really be the church in every way that Jesus has redeemed and called us to be. Then we would honor and glorify Him as well as act as true Ambassadors who represent and reveal Him to a lost and dying world.

If the "Come and See!" part of evangelism would match or exceed the "Go and tell!" there would be no lack of harvest. Rather than begging, bribing and trying to trick them to church, we might see thousands coming and saying, "What must I do to be saved so I can have what you have?" As we seek to be like Him and present the true Jesus as well as real Biblical Christianity to others, perhaps we will see an increase in radical conversions and true disciples filling our churches. This would be far more desirable than the man-centered methods and messages which draw people for what they can get from God, but result in many who have no desire or intention to surrender and serve God.

This brings me back to the questions from the last chapter because the people Jesus is coming back for are the same ones who are living for and seeking to honor and reveal Him now. To answer the question "Lord, what must I do to be one of the few who are chosen and received by you and to keep from being one of the many who are deceived and fall away in the last days?" The Lord clearly spoke that the key was to get and keep my heart right. He also added the command "Be quick to repent and quick to forgive!" When my heart is right it allows the Holy Spirit to lead me into all truth and away from error or deception. If my heart is not right, then another spirit will lead me away from God on a path of destruction.

The longer I walk with and serve the Lord, the more I am convinced that it all comes down to a matter of our heart and that the main responsibility of every follower of Christ is to get and keep his/her heart right. This will allow the Spirit to bring us into all God has for us – not only fully preparing us for His coming but mightily using us beforehand. However, even with the help of God and all that He has given us that pertains to life and godliness (Jesus, the Spirit, the Word…) this will be no easy matter. If our heart is the key, then our heart will be the place of the battle. The fact that our enemy, the devil, knows this truth is evident from our life as well as demonstrated throughout the whole history of mankind.

In his book Waking the Dead: The Glory of a Heart Fully Alive, John Eldredge very eloquently describes this battle over our heart. "Our life is the story of a long, brutal assault against our heart by an enemy who knows what we could be and fears us." "Since being all we can be, all God created and redeemed us to be, requires our whole heart, then it is essential that we get and keep our heart right. We get it right, first of all, when we receive Jesus as our Lord and Savior and He gives us a new heart that desires to please God rather than living to please ourselves. It is also necessary to ask Jesus to heal the broken places, even the deepest wounds inflicted by the enemy. This may be painful and take some time and help from both God and others depending on how deeply these hurts have been buried and how willing we are to open ourselves again to face these issues as we invited Jesus, the Healer, to come with us into these scary places.

Even after we have received a measure of healing for our heart, we must continually be on guard against the attacks of the devil. Proverbs says, "Guard your heart with all diligence, for from it flows the wellspring of life." Because all of our true life flows out of our heart (your innermost being, who you really are), we must expect it to be under constant assault from the enemy of our soul. His ultimate purpose is to turn our heart away from God and eventually cause us to worship and serve him. If he can't distract and deceive us with his lies and counterfeit/imitation blessings, he seeks to wound and discourage us to the point that we harden our hearts and therefore, cannot receive from God nor live for Him.

Besides diligently guarding our hearts, we must positively determine to set our hearts and minds on the things above. This requires a sincere desire and effort to put God and His kingdom first in everything so that nothing can draw us away from the Lord. Like Jesus, we can say, "the ruler of this world (Satan) is coming and he has nothing (no hook, foothold, open door) in Me." Is it possible to be so devoted and committed to God that our three-fold enemy (the flesh, the world and the devil) have little or no hold on us, or even appeal to us? This is the love that Jesus has for His Father, as well as us, and this is the love He is looking for in His bride the church.

Col. 3:1-2
Mt. 6:33
Jh. 14:30

3

It All Comes Down To Love!

That it all comes down to love should not be a surprise for anyone who knows God, His ways and His Word. In fact it is so clear that this is what He created and redeemed us for. I wonder how we can be so often and easily distracted from His intended purpose? The Bible declares that God IS love, and those who know Him even a little would not dispute that love is indeed, His very essence and nature. It was the overwhelming, unconditional, sacrificial, and everlasting love of God that brought me to Him. His love compels me to seek and serve, long for and live for, as well as to love and worship Him alone. As His love is poured out into my heart by the Holy Spirit more and more, I can more fully represent Him to others.

The Father demonstrated His love by giving us His very best gift, His only begotten Son and the salvation He came to release, so that we could be reconciled to a relationship and restored to our purpose in Him. What an amazing love that would entrust His precious Son into the hands of evil, cruel men who were subject to the control of the enemy, and then say it pleased the Lord to crush Jesus so that He could justify and bring many to salvation! Truly He has gone to great lengths to make a way for His rebellious, prodigal children to come back to Him, and no matter how far away we've strayed or what we've done on our wayward path, He is always ready to welcome us home. It was this forgiveness, this grace, this awesome love that literally

Is. 53:10-11

overwhelmed me for months after my conversion, and God is continually drawing me back to my first love.

Of course, Jesus is the perfect and ultimate expression of God's love for us, His children. Just His willingness to leave and lay aside the rights, privileges and glories of heaven (to empty Himself and become of no reputation) in order to come to earth and take on the form of man, is an amazing display of love and humility. This path, which I call the Divine Condescension, led Him lower still. From the helpless babe in a stinky stable, He became a servant and was fully obedient even to the painful, shameful, sacrificial death of the cross.

His life was a continuous message and revelation of God's love as He sought to fulfill His mission to seek and save the lost. What great compassion moved Him to preach the Good News and bring healing and deliverance, to destroy the works of the devil and set the captives free! Jesus was open to all who came in faith to His invitation, and was willing to reach out and touch the least and lowest, the rejects and outcasts of society. Even His strong rebukes to the religious leaders and their followers was meant to shock and turn them from the pride and deception that hardened their hearts and blinded their minds, to the life and love He wanted to give them.

If His life and message is not enough to convince us of God's love, then certainly His sacrificial death for us on the cross should leave no room for us to doubt. What kind of King, Lord, God would choose to suffer and die in such a brutal way (as accurately portrayed in the "Passion of Christ" movie by Mel Gibson) for people such as you and I? A love that would pay such a high price for the object of His love is incomprehensible, especially considering the condition of men. Paul eloquently states in Romans that a good man may die for a friend, family or righteous man, but Christ demonstrates God's love by dying for us while we were ungodly sinners and His enemies!

Rom. 5:6-10

As if all these expressions of God's love are not enough to persuade us and make us want to love and serve Him forever, God continues to lavish His love upon us. When you look around at the incredible beauty and variety of this world, which God created for our enjoyment, how can we keep from offering continuous praise and thanksgiving? Then, as you think of His daily protection and provision, even His strength and help in the midst of trials and tribulations, surely we should proclaim as

Ps. 63
Rom. 8:38-39

the psalmist, "Your loving kindness is better than life." No matter how good things around us may be or how bad they get, nothing compares to your awesome love and "nothing can separate us from the love of God which is in Christ Jesus our Lord." Such an amazing love deserves a strong and sincere response.

Once again I want to go back to questions in the first chapter: What kind of people is God looking for and preparing to be His Bride forever? Who is Jesus coming back for and will I be among them? In light of the profound and continuous love of God briefly outlined above, let me say, above all else, God desires, deserves and demands our wholehearted love. I will spend the remaining chapters of this book trying to share what this love is and isn't, ways it should be expressed, and to show at least a few of the blessings and benefits that come only to those who love Him.

Before I continue I want to emphasize two things. First, because it truly is a matter of the heart, our main responsibility is to get and keep our heart right with God. The second follows the first which is the fact that above all else, God desires, deserves and demands our wholehearted love. If you get nothing from this book, please meditate on these two truths and allow them to be fully established in your heart and mind.

4

God Desires, Deserves and Demands our Wholehearted Love

The fact that God desires our love is evident in the incredible lengths He went in making a way for us to come back into relationship and fellowship with Him after the rebellion and fall in the garden. What an amazing plan of salvation which was declared and instituted at that very moment (though I'm sure it was already in His mind long before) which would not only provide the way but also reveal the need and begin to draw His children back to Him. At the time of the fall, His plan began to unfold, and we can see with awe and thanksgiving that all of history is either a pointing toward or a flowing from the perfection of the life and death of Jesus Christ, the ultimate expression of God's love for us.

Gen. 3

Why would the God of the universe, the King of Kings and Lord of Lords, set me, set us as the object of His love? Knowing how far I had strayed from Him and His purpose for my life, I would not even have accepted me back, let alone wooing me and running to meet me when I finally came to the end of my selfish ways. Considering the mess I had made of my life and the many people I had hurt along the way, I was overwhelmed with the fact that He not only loved me now that I had "come to the end of myself", but that He had loved me all along, even when I was in the depths of my sin and rebellion. The experience of such an amazing, unconditional love was both incredibly freeing (from the performance trap) and profoundly motivating to want only to live for and enjoy Him and His love forever.

As I have come to know God in greater ways and consider the incredible magnitude, beauty and variety both of Him and the revelation of Himself in His creation, I am even more amazed that He would choose man to lavish His love upon. Though I know we were created in His image with the special purpose of fellowship with Him, I am also fully aware that without Him, without the breath of His life, I am a worm or dust, and can do nothing that will bear fruit for His eternal Kingdom. Like David, I wonder, "When I consider the heavens, the work of your fingers… what is man that you are mindful of him and the son of man that you visit (give attention to or care for) him?" He goes on to say in awe that God has, indeed, created us in His likeness both for fellowship and to rule and reign with Him.

Jn 15:5
Ps 8:3-6

By now, it should be quite clear that what God desires, what He is looking for in His people, is our wholehearted love. In addition to desiring our love, it should also be obvious that He undoubtedly deserves it. Just because of who He is alone, certainly He deserves our complete worship, devotion and surrender. There could not possibly be anyone or anything greater upon which to set our heart or affection. Since there is no god like our God, He alone is worthy of our wholehearted love and nothing else even comes close.

If reflecting upon all that He is somehow is not enough to convince you that God deserves your love, then meditating on all He has done and continues to do for us should. As we carefully consider His awesome plan for us, both in creation and redemption, it should lead us to give Him all the love He desires and deserves in appreciation for His wondrous works. Especially the length that He went to and the price that He paid to bring us back to Him after we rebelled and turned away, this should certainly capture our hearts.

It may appear that I am belaboring these points regarding how much God both desires and deserves our love, but I know how quickly we forget (just like the Israelites!) Even though we have the Spirit, the Word and our sacraments to help us remember God and all He has done for us, yet we are easily and often distracted by other things. Is it because we are so shortsighted that we only consider what we want and think we need at the moment, forgetting both the past blessings and future glory? Or are we, like the current free agent athlete, always looking for a better deal? The enemy of our soul is constantly trying

Ps. 106

to tell us what we want to hear in order to turn us away from God. However, his promises are either empty or come with strings attached, the price of which you don't want to pay!

Since God knows our weaknesses and how easily we can get discouraged, distracted and/or deceived, He made His desires clearly known in His Word, the Bible. Then to add emphasis, knowing that what He desires and deserves would not always be strong enough motivation for our love, He goes even further and demands wholehearted love. In response to a question about which is the greatest commandment Jesus replied, "You shall love the Lord your God with all your heart, soul, mind and strength." Then he quickly added a second commandment declaring that love for Him will be revealed and perfected in our love of others, and that everything comes down to these laws of love.

Mt. 22:37-40

For those who would be His people, true followers of Jesus Christ and the Bride for which He is returning, it has hopefully become clear by now that God not only desires and deserves but also requires and demands our wholehearted love. Upon this passage of scripture alone we can see that Jesus emphatically states that love is both the priority and summation of all that He desires and commands from those who are His.

There are many other places in the Word that both confirm and clarify this truth, which I will explore at length in the remaining chapters. By then it should become abundantly clear the kind of people Jesus is looking for, preparing, and expecting to find when he returns for His Bride and consummates His Kingdom on earth. First, however, it is necessary to understand the essence of true love which has been so lost and denigrated in our society today.

5

What Is True Love?

In the past few years I have had the privilege of performing more weddings than all of the previous years of ministry combined, including six of my own children! I can't help wondering why there has been such a large number that I have been involved with at this time. Is God trying to tell me and prepare me for something? Perhaps it was a way not only to get me thinking about preparing for the Great Wedding that is coming, but also it has stirred me to write this book in order that others might also be ready.

Anyway, before I will agree to do a wedding, I first ask if the couple is willing to do a series of preparation classes. This is a requirement for me to do the service since it is my desire and obligation to help them understand God's purposes for marriage, as well as give them some Biblical and practical principals to help them be successful.

Since love is what brought them together and to the place where they want to be together for the rest of their lives, much of our discussion starts with and revolves around the question: What is true love? I know that only by coming to a deep understanding of the answer, will their marriage have much hope to even survive (in a society where divorce is so easy and prevalent) let alone become the blessing and fulfillment they desire and dream of (and God intends for His children!)

For them to recognize the truth, however, it is first necessary to reveal the lie and debunk the Hollywood myth that so pervades our world through the media and has been perpetrated by the enemy to deceive and destroy God's children. It doesn't take a prophet or brilliant mind to come to this realization, only someone who is willing to honestly look around at the true condition of marriage and family in this nation. The destruction, as well as the anger, depression and confusion it brings, is evidence that the enemy has been quite successful in diverting untold millions from God's intended path of life and love. Even a fool would find it hard to deny this reality, and yet the depth of our deception is revealed in our unwillingness to even recognize let alone admit our true condition.

I was one of those blind, stubborn people whose selfishness and pride made me refuse to face the truth of the direction my life was heading until I fell off the cliff. It was through a very painful divorce that I realized I had hurt the people I loved the most (whom I was now losing), and I finally came to the end of myself and called out to God. I was amazed to find that He was there waiting for me with open arms in spite of the mess I had made of my life and the way I had hurt Him and others in the process.

When the Lord came into my life, I finally began to experience and understand what true love is since God is love. Through the divorce and many other experiences in life and ministry, God has tried to teach me how to love as He does. I was immediately thrust into a situation where I tried to love and be loving to someone who would not receive or even acknowledge my efforts, let alone appreciate and reciprocate.

These lessons have continued over the almost 30 years I have walked with the Lord, and I wish I could say I am now quick to and good at putting what I'm learning into practice. However, I must admit that I have often been slow to learn and obey these important truths. I can say in all honesty that I have made some progress, which shows you can teach an "old dog new tricks," but only if you're patient and don't expect him to perform quickly! Thank God for His incredible patience with us! May He continue to develop that same quality of love in us, toward ourselves, as well as others.

This leads me back to the couples I take through pre-marital counseling and our key question: What is true love? To help move them out of the Hollywood romantic delusion that so pervades our society and draw them toward a deeper understanding of a lasting, meaningful love, I often present them with a question based on two fictional scenarios. Which of these two stories represents real love to you?

The first begins with your favorite male actor knocking on the door of an apartment looking strikingly handsome with roses in one hand and a bottle of special wine in the other. Of course the door is opened by our favorite leading lady who is especially stunning in her very sexy and most revealing dress. There is perfume and romance in the air as we see the table is beautifully set and prepared with a gorgeous centerpiece and burning candles while the lights are perfectly dimmed. To add something to the already amazing atmosphere, we hear our most favorite romantic music playing softly in the background.

As he walks in, handing her the flowers and wine, she mentions that she has prepared a meal for this special occasion. The conversation that follows goes something like this:

"You look lovely tonight darling and the atmosphere is perfect. It's so good to see you again!"

She replies, "I've missed you so much. Why have you been away for so long?"

"Well, you know my work and busy schedule. It really keeps me tied up, and of course, I'm traveling all over the world. But it's great to be back here with you, and I'm sure we'll have a wonderful time together."

As she opens and pours each glass of wine, they sit down to a delicious meal. The conversation during the meal is friendly and light with the perfect touch of humor and grace but no real depth, no difficult questions that might lead to an argument. Let's just enjoy the moment! They finish their meal and enjoy another glass of wine together.

Then she smiles seductively and asks, "Would you like some of your favorite dessert?"

"Absolutely!" he replies and then picks her up and carries her off to the bedroom for a passionate time of lovemaking.

She wakes up the next morning as he is finishing getting dressed and preparing to leave.

"Do you have to go so soon?" she says with a trace of sadness and longing in her voice while trying not to sound too clingy or whiney.

"Sorry sweetheart, but you know that duty calls. Hopefully, I'll get back this way before too long. I really enjoyed our time together and hope we can do it again soon. Good bye and thanks for everything," he says as he walks out the door.

(We have all watched numerous scenes like this in movies or TV programs or read about it in books and magazines. While the details may be somewhat different, the message is pretty much the same: love is an exciting but fleeting feeling and experience, so grab for all the gusto you can get but don't expect it to last. This has left a trail of empty and broken hearts as people use each other to get their temporary "love" fix while becoming increasingly more selfish, cynical and hardened.)

The second scenario is in striking contrast to the first. It is quite bland and a little gross, hardly the things that dreams and fantasies are made of. You would probably have trouble selling tickets to a movie with this theme, although the second half to "The Notebook" gives a hint that this is the kind of love we desire in our heart.

Anyway, this story begins with an overweight middle aged married couple asleep at home in their queen-sized bed. It's a typical night – she's curled up in her comforter and flannel pajamas while he is on the other side in his underwear and only a sheet. Just a short time ago she had woken up from his snoring, so as always, she shook him and told him to rollover. Now, however, she wakes him up with a different and very urgent message:

"Honey, are you awake? I'm not feeling good. I think I'm going to throw up!"

"Well, you'd better head to the bathroom," he says groggily not realizing the seriousness of the situation.

She rolls over and tries to get up, but it's too late. As she vomits partly on the bed and the rest on the floor, he quickly rises to help. "Sorry," she says weakly as she staggers for the bathroom puking again in the hallway before she makes it to the toilet. He rushes to catch up, dodging the mess, and holds her forehead as she wretches violently a few more times removing the last traces of their evening meal as well as some stomach fluids.

Satisfied that she is finally done, she slowly stands up. He goes over to the sink to get her a warm washcloth to wash her face and a small glass of water to rinse her mouth. "Thanks", she mumbles still feeling tired and sickly. "That's ok, sweetheart, sorry to see you so sick. I know how much you hate to throw up," he adds affectionately touching her shoulder.

"I'm going to lie down on the couch," she says hurrying to get prone before it hits her again. He gets a blanket and her pillow and tries to make her as comfortable as possible before going back to clean up the mess. As he holds his breath to lessen the smell, he listens to hear if she needs him or gets up again. Finally, as he finishes changing the sheets and getting the bedroom wiped up, he smiles as he hears her snoring softly in the other room. He checks on her one more time before going back to bed and trying to sleep with his ears open so he can be ready if she needs help again in the night.

As I finish the second story, I ask them which story they think more accurately represents true love. Without exception they quickly and emphatically state that the latter story is the best example of real love (What would you say?) This leads to deeper discussions of true love and how it can be nourished and developed to the fullness.

6

Love is More Than A Feeling!

Since understanding and then walking in love is the key to fulfilling all God's purposes for our lives, I try to bring each couple in pre-marital counseling to a deeper realization of the essence of true love. In light of our previous stories, I then ask them whether true love is primarily a feeling, thought, or decision. Is the love God has for us and desires from us, as well as the love we desire from each other , found in the realm of the emotions, the mind or the will? They usually say very strongly it is a decision of the will and I further illustrate this point with the following story.

A man came to the church office one day and said very firmly, "Pastor, I don't love my wife anymore!" The pastor replied even more empathically, "Then you'd better start!" He was shocked, and thinking the pastor didn't understand, he began to explain.

"Our love has been growing colder over the last few years and it's to the point now that I have no feelings toward her at all. In fact I've begun to think that I actually married the wrong woman, and I've met someone who seems to understand me and has many of the same ideas that I do. I know that God's word speaks against divorce, but I think in this case it's best for everyone – don't you?"

The pastor could clearly see what the man wanted and that he had probably already made up his mind what he was going to do. In hope that the man really was looking for help and counsel (or at least he might still be open to it!) rather than sympathy and confirmation, the pastor decided to speak the truth and prayerfully trust God for the results.

"So you don't feel love for your wife anymore and you think you may have married the wrong woman?"

"Yeah, that's it exactly!" said the man realizing the pastor had truly understood and therefore would agree with his conclusions.

However, the pastor began to share the truth about real love that would lead to a much different ending. He explained that while feelings are certainly part of love, they are not the primary aspect. If they were, then considering how erratic and changeable emotions are, love would be something we fall into and out of quickly and often. Add to that our confused thoughts that are often shaped by the selfish mindset of the media, and it is no wonder marriages and our society is in such a mess.

Our primary pursuit has become our happiness, which we then define as having what we want. Love, then, in found is someone who makes me happy by giving me what I want. When our wants change or they are no longer meeting our needs for some reason, then we conclude that love has died. Then we begin looking around for something or someone else that will fulfill our wants and needs in order that we can be happy again.

The pastor then boldly declared that God hasn't left us to this empty and confusing pursuit of happiness, but has clearly defined the path of life and love through His word. Then to make this path possible, as well as perfectly demonstrate how to walk it out, He sent His Son, our Lord and Savior Jesus Christ. Choosing this path will mean we must walk differently than many people who are following their selfish, worldly pursuits. It means getting back to our intended purpose, that for which we were created and redeemed – to glorify God and enjoy His fellowship forever.

With that said, the pastor then asked the man a very direct question, "Do you want to glorify God and enjoy His presence in your life more than you want to do what you think will make you feel good? Is your relationship with Him and your desire to please Him more important than even what you think will make you happy? If so, what would God have you do in relation to your wife?"

"I guess He would want me to stay with her," The man replied somewhat reluctantly.

"Is it possible to show love, to do loving acts even when we don't feel love and our mind is full of confusing and conflicting thoughts?" asked the pastor.

"I suppose it is," said the man slowly beginning to see where this was heading.

"Then you'd better start!" said the pastor bringing them back to his original statement. "As we choose to love and be loving, hopefully the feelings will follow and we will remember the reasons we wanted to be together as well as the dreams we had for our future. It may take some time to heal the wounds and trust one another again, but at least you will have the peace of knowing you are seeking to honor and please God in your marriage. Eventually you will begin to experience His pleasure, which will release blessing and favor in your life and love."

"Thank you, pastor!" the man replied with a very sincere heart. "You have saved me from a huge mistake that would have had lasting consequences, perhaps even eternal! I'm going to stop spending time with the other woman and focus my time and energy on trying to restore my relationship with my wife. If God will help us forgive and get back, maybe we will get even stronger and closer to the purpose He has for us, so that we can glorify Him in our lives and marriage."

As I finish this story, I remind the couples that while it is fiction, the principles are true and will be played out in most marriages. The ending, however, is not always happy depending upon the choices made when they arrive at this place in their relationship. What holds you when the feelings begin to fade and your thoughts begin to travel to greener pastures? What keeps you together and helps you not only to go through, but grow from, the difficult times that inevitably come to every life and family?

7

Call My People To Commitment

I'm sorry if I've spent too much time sharing about my experiences with marriage counseling. It may seem that I am belaboring the point, but the theme of this writing is preparing the bride. Could it be that the key to our survival and fulfillment in marriage is the same quality of love that God desires, deserves and demands from His people and what Jesus will be looking for in His bride when He comes? Furthermore, developing this characteristic will not only strengthen and secure our relationship with God, but it will largely determine the depth and duration of almost everything that's important in life.

This brings me to what could have been another subtitle of this writing, which is also the commission the Lord gave me when He first called me into ministry; Call My People to Commitment. Commitment is the key, the glue that holds relationships together and allows them to grow and flourish even in troubled times. It is the essence of the love God has for us and that He desires and demands from us toward Him and others. (In fact, unless true love was found in the will how could it be the expected and commanded?)

One of the definitions of commitment in Webster's New World Dictionary is "to bind, as by a promise; pledge." God binds Himself to us in covenant which is the strongest kind of commitment, sealed in the blood first symbolically with animals until the perfection that would come in His Son Jesus Christ. Through this covenant He promises always to provide our needs and is committed to bringing us to the very best He has for us (even if we don't think we want it!). He pledges Himself to us forever that He will never leave us or forsake us and will always be with us and concerned for our well-being even to His own hurt.

In the world most of us have only experienced conditional, performance-based love, which lets us know that we are loved only "if' or "because" we meet certain needs or requirements. This keeps us feeling pressured and used but never really fulfilled until we experience God's unconditional love! What a freeing thought when we realize there's nothing we can do to make Him love us less or more, because His love isn't based on what we do! God loves us because of who we are (His children!) and because of who He is! God is love! He loves us not because we are worthy but "in spite of" our worse faults, which he knows more than anyone else, including ourselves. Jesus fully demonstrated this love when He died for rebellious sinners, who had chosen to be God's enemy, in order to make a way for us to once again come back to the Father.

Such an amazing love is pretty much beyond our ability to comprehend – it definitely sounds too good to be true! Though we may not be able to understand why God would be so passionately committed to people who would turn their backs on Him, those of us who have chosen to open our hearts and receive his love are quick to shout the truth of God's love! It truly is an act of faith to open your heart, to surrender and make yourself vulnerable after all the hurts and disappointments we've experience in life, but who is more worthy? He has boldly and often declared His love to us through His Word and His Son, which has been confirmed by many throughout history. Not only will He never let you down (though we don't always understand His ways), but you will find that only His love satisfies fully and forever.

Hopefully, by now you are convinced of God's incredible love and commitment toward us, His children, even if, for some strange reason, you have not yet fully received it for yourself. (What could possibly hold you back except the thief who wants only to keep us from receiving and walking in the fullness of the life, love and blessing that God has for us?) For those who have received His awesome love, it should be both our greatest desire and highest responsibility to share it with others and to give it back to Him. Why would we possibly consider doing otherwise?

The love and commitment God calls us to, though satisfying and fulfilling, is seldom easy. Often we are called to remain devoted to Him when we don't understand and definitely don't enjoy what He has allowed to come our way. Even more, it means obeying Him by showing His love to our enemies – those who speak hurtfully toward us and despite fully use us. We are required to remain committed to God and others even when it gets very difficult and painful.

We much prefer the easier kind of love – the romantic "days of wine and roses" – where everything is wonderful and we seldom have hassles. While such love is usually shallow and temporary, we can get in and get out without getting hurt. Thinking we are saving ourselves from heartache, we end up feeling more wounded, angry and empty than ever because we have turned away from the only perfect love that satisfies eternally.

Maybe you believe that God does indeed love us this deeply, but surely He wouldn't expect us to love Him and others as He loves us. After all, you may be thinking, we're only human! That lie from the enemy has become our greatest excuse for not loving as God desires, deserves and demands. The truth is that we have become partakers of the divine nature, and God is love! As we open our hearts to Him, His love comes into our life and is continued to be poured out in our life by the Holy Spirit as we ask and continue to walk with Him.

So, the answer is yes! God both desires and demands this wholehearted committed love from his children, and Jesus is looking for it in the Bride He is returning for. In fact, without this commitment we not only won't be prepared when He comes, but our relationship with him probably won't endure through the troubled times ahead. What He calls us to is not only His desire, but also is essential to fulfilling our purpose and destiny.

Because this call to commitment is so crucial not only to finishing our race, but also for being and doing all God desires of us, I will take the reminder of the book to further examine this theme. Using both scripture and personal experience I will describe some of the characteristics, as well as ways of developing and growing in this type of love, so that we will be ready when He comes.

I can almost hear Jesus asking us like He did Peter when He was about to leave the earth, "Do you love me more than these?" Bob Jones, who is recognized by many as an accurate prophet in our present day, went to heaven in a near death experience and said only one question was asked by Jesus, "Did you learn to love?" I believe those who prayerfully read these pages and seek to put these truths into practice with the help of the Holy Spirit will be ready to say joyfully, "Yes, Lord! You know that I have loved you and others as you desired, deserved and demanded from me."

II.

Characteristics of Commitment/ God's standard of Love

8

A New Commandment

In John chapter 13, Jesus takes the Father's Great Commandments to love God and others one step further. He gives us a new commandment that both ties the two together and adds a standard by which our love will be measured. Jesus states that love for others is the distinguishing quality of a true disciple, someone who has received Him as Lord and Savior and seeks to follow Him. In addition, He defines the kind of love He expects in His followers – we are called to love one another in the same manner in which He has loved us. The life and death of Jesus is the model and motivation, as well as the measure of all true love.

John also clearly makes these points in his first letter, that our love for God is revealed in our love for others and our love for others reveals that the love of God has been perfected in us. Furthermore, he states that the love of God as demonstrated through Jesus, is both the motivation and standard for our love toward one another. This is possible and expected only through those who are born of God and know God, as His very nature, which is love, has come to dwell within them.

What are your thoughts as you read these words of Jesus and John regarding love? If you're anything like me, when the reality of these truths hits you, the immediate reaction is a combination of "yeah, right!" and "help!" As we begin to understand the level of love and commitment God is calling us to, it is even more evident that we can't do it without Him.

I mean, loving others as Jesus loved me... that's just not going to happen even with my best efforts!

Fortunately, we don't have to do it alone. Whatever God commands us to do, He will also enable us to do. He has given us the Holy Spirit who is the Helper, the one who comes alongside of us to supply the grace that is needed. In fact, the Bible tells us He is working in us to give us the will and the way, the desire, as well as the wisdom and power, to please God. It must be remembered, however, that He requires our cooperation. We must put our efforts together with the Spirit to "work out our own salvation in fear and trembling." The fear is that we would fall short of the grace given to us, and due to our complacency, we would fail to honor and glorify God in the way He desires.

So, while we can't love in the way God desires and demands without His help, He won't do it without us. He has provided us with all that we need, but we must determine to lay hold of all that He has given us and make every effort to walk in love and commitment to God and others. If there's a failure in love, it's not God's fault. We are the ones who have dropped the ball, who have failed to receive and release God's love in the measure He desires and requires.

It's time! As we see the day drawing near and all that needs to be done to be prepared for His coming, truly we are being called to commitment.

II Pet. 3:11, 14

In light of who God is and all He has done for us, as well as the possible soon return of our Lord Jesus, what manner of persons ought we to be? How would we want to be found by Him? Surely, above all else, we should be passionately devoted to loving and faithfully serving the Lord! Where is the fire, the zeal that is so profoundly obvious in a bride preparing for her wedding? Could it be that we need a radical change of mind concerning both our current condition and our future destiny?

9

What Kind Of Bride Is Jesus Coming For?

Certainly there are other qualities that Jesus will be looking for in His bride, but all of them arise from and grow out of our passion for Christ. The Word makes it very evident that Jesus is coming for a pure bride, without a spot, wrinkle or blemish. She will desire to please her beloved in all things and seek to develop an inner beauty, the holiness of heart and spirit that is free of compromise and contamination from the world and/or the flesh. This requires a commitment to develop the heart attitude of Jesus that is represented and manifested through the fruit of the Spirit.

The Lord is also expecting to find a powerful bride when He returns rather than a weak, wimpy church holding on by our fingernails crying, "even so, come Lord Jesus!" Our passion and love for the Savior will keep us pressing in and violently advancing the Kingdom. Determined to follow our Master, we will courageously face all opposition, seeking to not only to overcome but to also destroy the works of the devil. This is a fearless people caring more about glorifying God than their own life, and charging the giants of the enemy in order to bring honor and praise to His name.

Lk. 16:16
Mt. 11:12

Finally, scripture tells us the Lord is looking for a productive bride. Our passionate love for Him should drive us to do anything and everything He calls us to do in these exciting last days. We will not be sitting in our comfortable pews waiting for Him to come while wasting our talents, time and gifts. Instead, we will be a people who are redeeming the time by looking for every opportunity to do the Master's will until He comes. Like Jesus, we will be busy about the Father's business, working as long as there is still light to finish completely all that He asks us to do. Those who know and love Him will be used to go forth and do great exploits until the day He returns. These are the good and faithful servants who will hear, "Well done!" and receive their promotion and rewards in the coming Kingdom.

I'm sure there are many other specific characteristics the Lord desires in His bride, but they would probably all fit into one of these general categories – 1.purity, 2.powerful, 3.productive and 4.passionate. Books could be written on each of these in order to fill in the details, but my purpose and calling is to focus on the latter. It is my deep conviction that our passionate love and commitment to Jesus must be the true motive for all that we do for Him. Without it our efforts will fall far short of the standard He demontrates in His life and describes in his word, and/or degenerate into the prideful dead works of the Pharisees.

Paul emphasizes this truth in his powerful chapter on the priority of love in I Corinthians 13, when he shows us the more excellent way. In this beloved passage, which is often read at weddings, he very beautifully describes the characteristics of this God kind of love, both what it is and what it isn't. Without this love he boldly declares that in spite of our impressive abilities and acts of faith or sacrifice, we gain nothing and we are nothing! Finally, he proclaims that love is the greatest of all the essential Christian virtues (because it is eternal since God is love, while faith becomes sight and hope becomes experience.)

If we agree that love and commitment are the essence of all God desires and all Jesus is coming for, then it certainly would be wise for us to carefully read and prayerfully seek to practice these characteristics that Paul so powerfully describes. Even better, since Jesus perfectly demonstrated this kind of love and our destiny is to be conformed to His image, we should pray and strive to be more like Him.

For such a transformation to take place in our lives, there first needs to be a change in our mindset. In Romans 12:2 Paul teaches that a carnal/worldly mindset will cause us to be conformed to the world's lifestyle, but when our mind is renewed by the Spirit and Word to a spiritual way of thinking, we will be transformed to a kingdom mindset and conformed to the King. This attitude or way of thinking is further described by Paul in Philippians 2.

Those who truly desire to be more like Jesus and walk in the love that He displayed, need to take time to pray over and live in these particular verses. Ask the Spirit to develop in you this same mind and attitude of Jesus Christ. Then ask Him to help you walk in these same qualities of love that so pleased the Father that He highly exalted Jesus and gave Him the Name above all names – King of kings and Lord of lords. The attitude Jesus displayed and the characteristics of love God desires, can be summed up as humility, servant hood, obedience and sacrifice.

Each of these qualities is important and necessary but there is a progression to them – one leads to another! This path that Jesus walked I call the Divine Condescension and the Downward Path to Exaltation. If we are to truly become like Jesus, we must follow Him on this same road becoming perfected in love as we go. This is the hard way that leads to love and life, which few find because they fail to understand that only through death comes new life, resurrection life, abundant and eternal life. We must, therefore "let this same mind be in us which was also in Christ Jesus," and allow the Holy Spirit to develop this mindset in us so that the character will follow.

Mt. 7:13-14

10

God Gives Grace to the Humble

Knowing that I have been a pastor for many years, people often ask me which Christian virtue is most important to cultivate in order to please God. At first I would go through the list of all the significant possibilities – i.e. faith, hope, love, joy, peace, etc – but I always came back to humility. Since God gives grace to the humble and everything we do for Him requires grace, it stands to reason that we should seek to develop a humble heart.

In Philippians 2:3 God through Paul commands us "in lowliness of mind let each esteem others better than ourselves." This is a quality of true love that we seldom see in the world today. It was the same attitude that Jesus so profoundly displayed when He emptied Himself of all His heavenly rights, privileges and glory in order to come to earth and take the likeness of man. He did not come as an earthly king but as a helpless babe born in a smelly stable, letting go of His position of co-equal with God to make Himself of no reputation. Many people have never really meditated on the incredible love and humility that was required just to get Jesus from the glories of heaven to the mess of earth.

Jesus challenges His disciples to do just that when He commands us to take His yoke upon us, to fully submit to and walk with Him, in order to really learn from Him how to be meek and lowly in heart. In this way we will find rest for our soul – it is in humble surrender to our Beloved that we cease from our prideful striving to be in control and enter into the Lord's rest. Trust and surrender is required to love since it can only be entered into but can't be controlled.

It is this attitude of humility that will bring the oneness, the unity that God desires with and among His children. Contention, Proverbs tells us, comes only through pride. How many arguments and decisions come simply to prove we're right and/or better than the others? How many times do we say to God (or at least imply) that we know better than He does what's good for us, having convinced ourselves that what we want is really best even if He clearly states otherwise?

Prov. 13:10

Many today, as in Jesus' time, continue to do what they want, even claiming to do it for God, but they will have a huge awakening on the day Jesus returns. In response to their proud boasting of all they did for Him, Jesus will declare to them, "I never knew you, depart from me, you who practice lawlessness." Only those who humbly submit to His Lordship and lovingly commit to doing His will, may enter the Kingdom of Heaven.

Mt. 7:22-23

When His disciples wanted to know "who is greatest in the Kingdom of Heaven," Jesus made a very shocking statement. He set a child in their midst and assured them that unless they (changed their mindset) to be like a child they couldn't enter the Kingdom. Then He went on to tell them that those who humble themselves to become as simple and trusting as a child will receive the fullness of the kingdom. Humility, then, which is acknowledging we are poor in spirit (or what Paul calls boasting of our weakness), makes God's all sufficient grace and all the resources of heaven available to us.

Mt. 5:2
II Cor. 12

Preparing ourselves for Jesus' coming starts by realizing that we cannot love nor do anything else He desires of us without His help. Further, we must understand that the grace we need (which is God's underserved favor, power and provision) comes only to those with a humble and contrite heart. Scripture goes on to say that God Himself actually resists the proud. So, why is true humility so rare and hard to come by?

Jn. 15:5

The real problem is that pride is such a persistent and subtle deception. It's persistent in that as soon as we think we deal with it in one area, it seems to pop up in three other places. Like dandelions on your lawn, unless we get down to the root of it, they keep coming back even stronger. Pride is subtle in that it can disguise itself as insecurity, a low self-image or even a false humility. However, it will eventually show its true colors, as with the case of King Saul and will lead to a downward path of destruction. Finally, it is deceptive in that pride is a lie from the enemy who wants us to fall as he did. The truth is clearly stated by Paul when he says, "I know that in me, that is my flesh, dwells no good thing."

Our attitude must be the same as Jesus when He came in humility and complete surrender to the Father. He stated that He could do nothing of Himself but only did what He saw His Father doing and only said what He heard His Father saying. Therefore, He could boldly declare that He always did what pleased the Father. We may not reach that same level of obedience but our motivation should be the same. As we humbly submit and devotedly commit our lives to Him, we can honestly say that our desire and determination is to always do what pleases Jesus.

While love in its essence is the humble surrender and commitment of our lives to another, this leads to action that further demonstrates the depth of our love. More than an emotion, love is a decision that must be shown through unselfish actions. This leads us to servant hood which was modeled by Jesus throughout His life on earth.

Because humility is so crucial not only to receiving all God has for us and fulfilling our destiny but even for our survival as a Christian. We are commanded in scripture to "humble yourselves under the mighty hand of God." This is done largely through serving and giving without thought of what will be received in return as we will see in the next chapter. Of course if we are unwilling to fall on the Rock to be broken, to submit our lives to Jesus in total surrender and service, the Rock will fall on us to crush our pride and self-sufficiency.

I Pet. 5:6

I was one of those prideful ones who had to come the hard way because I was so convinced that I was smart and strong enough to handle whatever came my way. The crushing came through my divorce when I thought I might go crazy or commit suicide, but finally realizing I was lost, I called out to the Savior. While I don't recommend coming this way, it does have a positive side in that you learn a lesson you don't soon forget. In fact, I pray often that God will give me a humble heart and teachable spirit so that I am not like "the stubborn mule that must be curbed with bit and bridle." Also, I look for opportunities to serve, especially asking for the least desirable tasks that few would choose.

Ps. 32:9

11

Developing the Heart of a Servant

There is a place in scripture where the mother of James and John, two of Jesus' disciples, comes to ask Him to give her sons positions of honor in His Kingdom. After describing the level of commitment it requires (the willingness to suffer and even die as He would), He further states that such places of authority are only for those for whom it is prepared by His Father.

Mt. 20:20-28

As soon as the other disciples hear about the request, they become very upset (probably because they desired the favored position!) Rather than rebuking them all for a self-seeking attitude, He uses the situation to teach them an important principle of the Kingdom.

Jesus began by contrasting the ways of the world with the mindset of the Kingdom, knowing that only a radical change in their thinking could prepare them for God's purposes. Unlike the leaders of the Gentiles who are quick to remind others of their position and show them who is boss, followers of Christ are called to be servants. Those who desire to be first or the greatest must actually choose to become the last and the least.

To emphasize this point Jesus uses His own life as the example and standard. He, being the Son of Man (A Messianic title), did not come to be served, but to serve and to willingly give His life completely in order to pay the price necessary to release others from slavery to sin. This further contrasts true servanthood as different than slavery, which is done out of duty and obligation without any real choice.

The true heart of a servant is revealed also in the Old Testament description of a bondservant, who willingly chose to serve his master rather than receive his freedom. His attitude came out of his love for the master and because he considered it a blessing and privilege to serve one so caring and highly esteemed. It was clear to him that he and his family were much better off with His master than out on his own, so he laid down his right to go free.

It is the spirit of giving that is modeled by Jesus and the attitude He requires of His followers. The desire of a true servant is to do more than what is asked or required. He will look for every opportunity to help with a need or simply be a blessing to His master without concern for recognition or reward. While it is true that God does reward us for every act of kindness done in His name and for His glory, our motive should be simply to please and honor Him because He is worthy and we love Him. What great lengths and depths will one go to show his love to another?

Again, Jesus further demonstrates the attitude of a servant in John 13 when He washes the disciple's feet. After eating their last meal together, He declares His total commitment to them (and to us), even the one who would betray Him, by His willingness to die in our place and shed His blood for our forgiveness. Further, He calls them to a life of commitment by teaching them a lesson on humility and selfless service. Washing the guests' feet was a very menial and distasteful task performed by a lowly servant, necessary because of the dusty roads littered with animal waste. Since there was no servant and none of his disciples assumed the role, Jesus laid aside His position as Teacher and Lord to show them true love through service.

In order to leave no doubt, He then states that His act of service is done as an example that they should follow. In learning to serve by taking the lowest place and dirtiest job of washing feet, they will receive a blessing and be truly following their Master's instructions and lifestyle.

Brother Lawrence, who was a cook in a monastery in the 17th Century, beautifully describes this attitude in the classic Practicing the Presence of God. He declares that he determined to do everything in a way that would please and show his love for God. For him the worst jobs became the best opportunity to demonstrate his love for the Lord.

Just think for a moment what a great marriage you could have if both people had this attitude of serving. Can you imagine what an awesome love would grow as they each looked for opportunities to help and bless one another, willing even to do the worst tasks (like cleaning toilets, changing diapers, scrubbing pots and pans, etc.) ? Jesus can and He's looking forward to coming for a bride that will share His love through committed selfless service for all eternity.

For most of us, however, this kind of giving and serving does not come easy. Besides the selfish nature we all inherited and practiced for many years before coming to Christ, our personality and training can add to our desire and determination to get our own way. Unless we are transformed by having our minds renewed by the Spirit and Word, the true heart of a servant is far from us, seems quite foreign to our nature.

Only as we open our hearts to Jesus and allow Him to rule in our lives can we begin to see this kind of love develop and grow. Then we begin to express our love in the way that God desires rather than picking and choosing how and when we want to show love. Again, Jesus is our example in His attitude of obedience to the Father.

12

Obedience and Commitment

Many people are willing to serve on their own terms at least for short periods of time. As long as it's convenient and not too uncomfortable, we can usually hang in there for certain tasks and a reasonable length of time. But please don't expect me to be there for the long haul, especially if the job gets messy. A little bit of that kind of service should go a long way toward endearing us to God and others.

Maybe we should begin to evaluate love and commitment in relation to our willingness to do what we're asked and we say we will do. Is obedience a quality of love and commitment that God is looking for in His people and Jesus expects from His followers? Certainly Jesus leaves no doubt when he asks, "Why do you call me 'Lord, Lord' and not do the things which I say?" In other words, it's not consistent to say we are committed and submitted to His authority if we are not obedient to Him. To use the term "Lord" without the consequent action is a contradiction and proves our declaration to be false. (Without the demonstration our proclamation will not get us an invitation to the celebration!)

Lk. 6:46 Mt. 7:21 Jn 14:15

Jesus speaks this truth another way when He tells His follows, "If you love me, you will keep my commandments." He is making it perfectly clear that those who say they love Him will be devoted to doing what He asks and expects of them. Their willing obedience will come from a desire to please Him rather than simply being an obligation or duty.

But what level of obedience does the Lord desire and expect from those who claim to love Him? If you're looking for an easier way, then by all means don't look at Jesus' life or pay attention to His words. Remember that His love and commitment to His Father and us took Him from the glories of heaven to the trials and labor of service and all the way to the brutal death on the cross. He gave Himself completely for us – would we expect or even want to give him anything less?

Our commitment to Jesus, then, finds its full expression through our immediate and complete obedience. To settle for anything less, while it may be easier and cheaper, would not be biblical Christianity nor would it be worthy of our beloved Lord Jesus. Yet, that is exactly what we often find ourselves doing.

Even now it hurts me to think of the many times I have disappointed the Lord with my lack of obedience. Maybe I didn't completely ignore His commands but my response was often delayed and/or only a half hearted, partial fulfillment of His request. It reminds me of the way I frequently acted toward my parents which of course, I also reaped from my own children.

Selective or partial obedience must be seen for what it is: disobedience and, therefore, sin or rebellion. Regardless of our good excuses for not doing what God asks (and I have an endless supply of them!), He still views it as a transgression of His command and an attitude of iniquity. The story of King Saul should be a great warning to us. While he was proud of his 99% obedience and sure it would impress God, Samuel gave a different message from the Lord and the kingdom was stripped from him. He made it clear that God is looking for those whose heart's desire is to please Him above all else.

Saul's example is such a contrast to the Lord's words and actions. Jesus continuously declared His purpose on earth was simply to do the will of the Father. At one point He even made the statement that His very food was "to do the will of Him who sent me and to finish the work." Obedience to the Father was even more important than our necessary food and Jesus could not consider stopping until the work was finished. At Gethsemane, realizing He would take on the sins of the world and become everything His Father hated, He did go so far as to ask if His assignment could somehow be modified. However, He was quick to add, "Nevertheless, not my will but thine be done." We

Jn. 4:34

are forever grateful that He was willing to be obedient to the end so that He could joyfully proclaim, "It is finished!"

Paul is another example of someone who wanted only to be completely obedient to the "heavenly vision" that He was given after His conversion. In the latter years of his ministry when faced with imprisonment or death, he boldly declared, "none of these things move me; nor do I count my life as dear to myself, so that I may finish my race with joy, and the ministry which I received from the Lord Jesus." Because Paul's desire was only to please and magnify Jesus (whether by life or death), he was able to make it to the end through many trials and tribulations knowing he had "fought the good fight, finished the race, and kept the faith." He was also confident that he, and all who show their love through obedient service until He comes, will be rewarded.

Acts 20:24
Phil. 1:20
II Tim. 4:7,8

Are we the kind of people "who have loved His appearing" and therefore are making every effort to be ready when He comes? Obedience is a very significant way for us to show our love and prepare us for His return. Scripture tells us, "blessed is the man who the Master finds doing His will when He comes." Perhaps this is a good time to recommit ourselves to seeking His will and completely obeying everything He ask us to do!

This must begin with taking the time to intently listen so that we may hear His voice (he who has an ear let him hear!) with the determination to be obedient no matter what He requires of us. Then we must get going! Like me with writing this book, stop procrastinating, waiting for that more convenient time which seldom comes and we've usually forgotten even if it finally does arrive. Determine to start, and ask the Lord for wisdom and grace to finish the work no matter how long and difficult the process may be.

Just as obedience is a characteristic of commitment, commitment is also necessary for complete obedience. Certainly that was true of Jesus when you consider the difficult road He travelled that eventually led Him up a hill called Calvary. Is it possible that we are also being called to a similar journey that leads to the ultimate commitment?

13

No Greater Love. . . Sacrifice

In this section we have been looking at some of the chief characteristics of commitment as demonstrated by our Lord and described by Paul in Philippians 2. As the model of the perfect love that God is seeking from us, Jesus took a very different attitude and path than we see in the world around us, (which is to do only what we have to do in order to get what we want.) God's love is concerned only about the well being of the other and focuses on giving even when it hurts and doing what's right even though it may not be received, appreciated or rewarded.

This kind of love takes a downward path of humility, servant hood, obedience and sacrifice. For us to follow our Lord's example and walk in the love He desires and requires, we must allow the Holy Spirit to change our mindset and attitude to be the same as Jesus. This is especially true of the final stage, since the spirit of sacrifice is opposite of the lifestyle we see and glorify in our present society.

While an occasional act of sacrifice in crises is considered honorable, a lifestyle of sacrifice in normal circumstances is more to be mocked and pitied. Even motherhood, which was once held in high esteem as an example of sacrifice, is now viewed as a deception and bondage from which we must be liberated. And the death of a soldier is often portrayed as a sad and senseless act to be mocked and vilified on our bumper stickers. We may respect people like Mother Teresa for their life of service, but few would view it as a way of life to be envied and emulated. No, our desire and prayer is more often to be like the rich and famous as glamorized by the movie stars, athletes, rock stars and even some of our favorite TV preachers.

Jesus, however, had a much different opinion of sacrifice as a demonstration of true love and commitment. He unashamedly called it the greatest kind of love when we "lay down our life for our friends," and commanded His followers to love one another in this same manner which He so beautifully demonstrated through His life and death. Nowhere do we see Jesus seeking or demanding something for Himself. His desire was always to please and honor the Father by revealing and sharing His love with all who would come. Even in times of weariness Jesus did not complain when people interrupted His attempts to rest, but he compassionately reached out to meet their needs.

Does Jesus desire and expect this sacrificial love from His disciples, from those He is coming for to receive as His bride? Well, think of it this way... would you want to marry a stranger or someone with whom you had a close friendship? Of course we would quickly choose the latter, and many have danced and sang the popular song, "I am a Friend of God!" While it's true that the Lord wants to draw us into an increasingly more intimate relationship and He has clearly shown that He is our "friend that sticks closer than a brother," have we really sought to be His friend?

We may casually claim to have many "friends," but usually we are very careful who we choose as true friends. They are the ones who have loved us in spite of our shortcomings and stayed committed to us even in the hard times. These are people we can trust and count on even when it's not comfortable or convenient. The truth is that we are fortunate to have a few people we can call good friends, those who are committed enough to possibly lay down their lives for us. So it should be with Jesus...

Lk. 9:23

He is looking for these who will "deny themselves, take up their cross daily, and follow Him." Really this is basic Christianity, but we have not preached true discipleship. Jesus really does expect His followers to lay down their lives – their dreams, wants, rights, etc. – in order to take up His life and purposes. He didn't come to make our life better but to give us a whole new way of living. That means embracing His will and walking His way, believing it is the best way, the right way, and the only way to real joy, peace, satisfaction and fulfillment.

Many in their excitement and amazement at the Lord's love and mercy start out this way – willing to do anything and everything He asks in order to please Him. But just like a marriage, the fires begin to die out as the inevitable testing comes. What do we do when things get difficult and confusing, or when Jesus challenges us to deeper levels of commitment and surrender, or when circumstances come our way that we don't understand and certainly didn't want?

It is how we respond in these very difficult and challenging times that determine our suitability to be a friend of God and eventually the bride of Christ. Will we determine to stay committed to Him and keep going forward even when many around us are backing off or walking away? Are we the kind of people who will say, "Lord, my life is yours. Do with it whatever you desire" even when His will seems very difficult to do or even understand? Can we in the midst of very painful and confusing trials when our flesh cries out for deliverance, still say, "though He slay me, yet will I trust Him" or "for me, to live is Christ and to die is gain' or "even if He doesn't deliver me, I will still love and serve Him because He is worthy."

Jesus undoubtedly deserves and is preparing such a bride for the Day of His coming. People who are passionately in love and committed to Him are ready and consider it a joy and privilege to live and even die for Him. The spirit of sacrifice is so firmly established in their lifestyles that there would be no question or hesitation in making the ultimate offering of laying down their lives for their beloved Savior and Lord. Like the first disciples, it would be considered a matter of rejoicing to be called to suffer or even die for His name.

It has been said that only something worth dying for is truly worth living for. Certainly our blessed Savior and soon coming King, the One who gave Himself completely for us, is worthy of a life of sacrifice. If some people in our world are willing to blow themselves up for a lie they believe, we should be totally committed to what we know to be the truth.

The early Christians had no trouble with this, and suffered great persecution and often martyrdom for serving the lord. Throughout history there have always been people who were willing to radically live for Jesus even to the point of laying down their lives. In our world today according to "Voice of the Martyrs" there are hundreds of thousands of people dying for their faith in Christ. Yet in our country, where such sacrifice is unnecessary because of our freedom to express our faith, many find it hard to be bold in their witness for fear they might be mocked, ridiculed and/ or rejected by others.

Perhaps in America our blessings have become a curse. That is to say, it has been so easy to be a Christian that we tend to avoid the hard tings.

We have received such abundant blessings for so long that we can't imagine the Lord would expect us to suffer for Him. Therefore, we have developed a convenient theology that speaks mainly of the blessings with little or no mention of responsibility and commitment. In many churches Christianity is presented as a kind of "bless me club" – come to Jesus for all He wants to do for you. He will continue to bless us right up to the time when things start getting tough, and then He will take us out of here!

Doesn't that sound like a great deal? Who wouldn't want to at least give it a try when we present it that way – a "seeker sensitive, man-centered gospel?" It is all about me, after all, and it's nice to know that even God is here for me. Maybe Jesus can help me get all the things I desire and deserve.

Sadly, many of the Christians sitting in our churches today have been drawn in by this approach. As long as I can get what I want (or at least I am made to believe that I can), and of course, I must also enjoy the service (keep me entertained), then I will try to stick with it, unless something better comes along. However, it may be hard to keep them if and when the difficult times come in our lives and the world, which is exactly what the Bible predicts will happen before the coming of the Lord – the great falling away from faith.

In our society of cheap, no-fault divorce and the free agent mentality, who will endure to the end? We have made it so easy to run from our commitments that it is now almost an epidemic in America. Most consider it normal and even wise to be continuously looking for a better deal and think nothing of walking away from a previous promise or contract, especially when things aren't going the way we want or think they should go. If God just wants me to be happy, then He certainly wouldn't want me to suffer, and of course, He would be in favor of the better deal!

I believe that is why many will be deceived and fall away from the faith in the last days. When offered the choice between suffering for Christ or receiving the provisions of the anti-Christ world system, how many will stay committed to Jesus no matter what comes? Only those who have settled it in their heart and truly love Jesus more than anything, anyone or even their own lives. Like the Psalmist, they have decided "His love is better than this life." They will not be overcome because they have already died to themselves, because they are baptized in the blood of the Lamb, and because they have declared their total commitment to Him and have not loved their lives even unto death.

Loving God with our whole heart so that we are committed to live and/or die for Him, is not only for His sake. As we approach the Day of our Lord's return and the perilous times that will precede it, only our strong committed love and complete trust in His love will hold us. If we will be one of the few who are chosen, who love Him to the end and have prepared our hearts for His coming, then cultivating our love for Him is definitely the key. For this we must understand what part is His and what is ours to do. Since love is a decision and action, more than simply an emotion, we must realize what God desires and requires of us. At the same time we must be perfectly clear that we could never love Him (or do anything of eternal value) without asking for and allowing Him to help.

Rev. 12:11

The love God is looking for requires us to be redeemed and restored to His original intention. We were created in the image of God and since God is love, we were therefore created in love, by love and for love. However, since the fall in the garden, our relationship with him was broken and our love has largely been tainted by sin or selfishness. All of history has been God's plan unfolding to fully bring us back to His loving purpose. The fact that it has taken so long is due only to how far we have fallen and our unwillingness to cooperate rather than God's desire or willingness to help.

Is it possible that we are the people who will see and be a part of the final scene, the consummation of His glorious plan at the end of the age? It may well be the case for those who recognize the signs of the times and are making every effort to cooperate with God in order to be the bride who has made herself ready. Those who are looking and longing for His coming so that they are continually preparing for His arrival can actually hasten the Day of His return! What can we do to not only be prepared, but even cause that glorious Day to come soon?

III: Cultivating our Love for and Commitment to God

14

Do You Really Love Me?

If love is what we were created for, redeemed for and what Jesus is coming for, then it is definitely time to ask ourselves, "Do I really love God?" Most who call themselves Christians would be quick to answer an emphatic, "Yes!" However, in light of some of the characteristics of love and commitment demonstrated by our beloved Savior and discussed in the previous section, perhaps we need to carefully consider our response. Do my attitude and actions truly reflect a deep love for my Lord?

I am reminded of the time that Jesus questions Peter, who would become a leader of the early church, "Peter, do you (agape) love me?" Many conclude that by asking it three times Jesus was seeking to bring restoration after Peter's threefold denial in his time of testing. Remember that Peter had previously declared his total commitment to Jesus and his willingness to follow and even to die for Him. In the face of his failure he now can at best claim a (phileo) friendship kind of affection, and even then, he could only trust in the Lord's divine knowledge as to the sincerity of his love.

Jn. 21:15-17

This was a very crucial time in that Jesus was about to be taken up from the earth and leave the work He had done at such a high cost in the hands of his imperfect followers. Could it be that Jesus was not only causing Peter to fully realize the deficiency of his love but also challenging him to a deeper level of commitment? Perhaps He is also doing the same for us at this time as we watch and prepare for His soon return.

Jesus went on to remind Peter to simply and wholly follow Him. In the past he had chosen his own direction and actions, but now Peter would need to completely surrender to the will of his Master and to willingly lay down his life. This would require him to follow his own individual call to discipleship and not compare or concern himself about another. The demand for loving obedience is the same for everyone and requires our total focus and submission. It's not enough just to casually say that we love God- our attitudes and actions must show our devotion to Him.

I believe now is the time to ask ourselves, "Do I really love God?" and then be willing to carefully and honestly reply. So much is riding on our answer that it is absolutely crucial for us to be ready to make the necessary changes if we cannot confidently reply, "yes, Lord, you know that I love you!" In light of the imminence of His return to receive His bride, this is certainly not an hour to be playing religious games or pretending to be something we're not. Jesus can obviously see through it (just ask the Pharisees!) and so can those around us, especially family and friends.

Perhaps, then, it would be better to ask the people closest to us if they think our lives are a good example of someone who really loves God. Since we can see the "speck in our brother's eye but not the log in our own." They are probably more aware of our shortcomings than we are. Challenge them to be brutally honest and specific about what they see and be willing to ask them for suggestions as to what and how to change. This may seem too radical but how much do we want to be one that the Lord receives and takes to be with Him forever on that Day? What are we willing to do in order to be ready for His coming?

Most of us are too good at rationalizing or justifying our behavior (and, therefore, deceiving ourselves) to leave something so important to our own best judgment. This is one time where we definitely need some help from our friends! Of course, God is also at work preparing His bride. We need to listen and obey what He is saying to His church in this urgent hour.

15

You Have Left Your First Love!

One theme I have heard over and over as I have communicated with pastors and believers from many persuasions is the need to get back to the simplicity of Christ. It seems like the church of today has gotten caught up in doing things, some of which are even for Jesus, but we have lost the sense of simply enjoying and following Him. Many have substituted a form of religion that is complete with rules and/or rituals, while getting further from and some even denying the power of a personal relationship. We're still doing religious deeds and feeling pretty good about it, but all the while there is a nagging sense that we have grown distant from the One we claim to love and serve.

This is where I found myself recently and is one of the factors that led to the writing of this book. After over 25 years of starting and pastoring churches, training up leaders and laborers, networking pastors and churches throughout the region, in addition to evangelizing and discipling many in Christ, I found myself feeling frustrated and empty. As I began to gradually pull back from my long list of activities and responsibilities, the Lord was finally able to speak to me so that I could hear – "you have left your first love!"

At first I was shocked and a little angry that He would say such a thing to me. After all, wasn't I sacrificing and doing all of this for Him? How could He possibly imply, in spite of all my efforts and accomplishments, that I had lost my love for Him? But the more I began to think about it and allow His words to really sink into my heart, the more I was convicted. I finally realized not only that it was true but, more importantly, it was exactly what I needed to hear. As I write these words I am once again amazed at both the immediate and far reaching benefit of His truth.

Like the church of Ephesus in Revelation 2, Jesus has commended some of my work done for Him, at least what was done with pure and proper motives. However, it was disappointing for me to see that I had left my determined priority and His greatest desire, which is love, substituting responsibility for relationship. I guess that explains the emptiness and frustration in my heat that I was too busy to fully recognize or that I was trying to ignore.

Could this also be the condition of the church in America at the very time in which we should be prepared for the Lord's return? As I take a moment to ponder this question, I can't help thinking there is much to do in order to get ready and so little time. I feel an urgency to get this written knowing it is probably at least two years late in getting started. While we know the Lord is moving to help prepare us, what can we do to cultivate our love and commitment to Him?

The remedy the Lord prescribes to the loveless church at Ephesus is also very appropriate for the American church at this time. In fact, having been married now for over 25 years, it applies to most marriages and relationships after a few years. Isn't it amazing (almost scary!) how quickly and often we can settle into comfortable routines and patterns while the excitement and romance slowly fades? We can get so busy doing things, even good things, that we don't realize our heart is growing cold and our reason for doing it has become a distant memory. How is it that we can feel so good about our work while at the same time feeling so far away from the One for whom we labor?

Jesus' challenge to those who have left their first love can be summed up in three words – Remember, Repent and Return. Our way back to Him and the love He desires from us starts by reminding ourselves how it was when we first met Jesus. Do you still think about and vividly remember the time when you were first saved from the path of darkness and destruction, and Jesus brought you into light and life? How soon we forget the incredible joy and thanksgiving that flowed form our hearts and lips not only for the awesome gift of salvation, but especially for the price He paid for it.

Knowing our human tendency toward selfishness and shortsightedness (what have you done for me lately, Jesus?), the Lord instituted the sacrament of Communion on the very night in which he was betrayed by one of His close followers. It was intended to be a continuous reminder of His amazing sacrificial love for us so that we would stay close to Him until He comes. Unfortunately, many of us have also betrayed Him by substituting and worshipping the symbol rather than the reality, and have allowed the precious covenant meal to degenerate into a mindless ritual rather than a meaningful connection with our Beloved.

16

He Who is Forgiven Much, Loves Much!

Throughout the New Testament Jesus teaches the people about the kind of love He desires, and He seeks to bring them to that place of deep intimacy and complete surrender. In one instance He had gone to the home of a Pharisee to eat with him, which was an act of covenant commitment in their culture and time. His willingness to accept the invitation shows His openness and deep love for all people, even those whose beliefs and hard hearted attitudes often led to some rather heated exchanges. It was their stubborn clinging to a religious system and the status it afforded them, rather than opening their hearts to the One they claimed to be waiting for, that angered Jesus. His strong words were meant to break the bondage and deception off of their lives so they could receive the life and freedom He came to bring, and then lead others to the One who sets our hearts free to love.

During this exclusive little dinner, someone decided to crash the party, which provided a perfect opportunity for Jesus to talk about the kind of love He is looking for. The intruder was a woman of ill-repute from the city (probably a prostitute) who was easily recognized as being from the opposite end of the socio-economic and religious end of the spectrum than the Pharisee. Her actions also provided a sharp contrast to that of Simon, which opened the door for the Lord to share an important lesson about love and forgiveness.

While Simon offered only minimal hospitality the woman poured out extravagant love and devotion to the Lord. She began by washing His feet with her tears and wiping them with her hair. Then she proceeded to kiss His feet and anoint them with the fragrant oil she had brought in her alabaster flask. Such an amazing display of love brought only disgust from the Pharisee who couldn't imagine how Jesus, if He were really a prophet, would allow such a woman to even touch Him.

Jesus knew his thoughts and attitude, so He responded by telling a story of two debtors. One owed a large amount while the other owed only a little but neither could repay, so both were freely forgiven their debts. Then Jesus asked a very significant question, "Which of them will love him more?" The Pharisee rightly answered, "I suppose the one whom he forgave more," which led to Jesus giving Simon a lesson about love and forgiveness. In contrasting the woman's actions and attitude with his, Jesus reveals that the depth of our love for Him will be in direct proportion to our realization of the magnitude of his forgiveness.

Perhaps this is where those of us who came out of a life of deep sin, like this woman of questionable character, have an advantage over those who have grown up in Christian or even good, moral families. When the depth of sin and selfishness in our heart has been manifested in obvious ways, it is pretty difficult to hold onto any illusion of our own goodness. That is even more evident when we stand in the light of the Lord's perfection, who was tempted as we are in every way, yet without sin. The experience of His love and forgiveness, knowing how short we fall from His example and standard, brings a response of overwhelming gratitude and devotion.

This lesson from scripture provides us with a key to cultivating a deep love and commitment for Jesus. Those who love Him much will know and remember both who He is and who we are without Him. The knowledge of His amazing love and forgiveness for sinful people, such as us, should be enough to make us desire to love and live for Him forever.

If you have not yet seen yourself as a gross sinner, if you still think of yourself as a pretty good person who made a few mistakes, I want to challenge you to do something very risky. Ask the Lord to show you how He sees you apart from Him. I was naïve enough to do this very early in my walk with the Lord and what He showed me shattered every illusion and self-deception of my true heart condition. He proceeded to roll the film of my life, which revealed more selfishness, rebellion and evil (as well as the hurt I had caused others) than I was prepared to handle. However, it brought me to a time of deep repentance and brokenness, which created a true and lasting conversion.

Perhaps it is enough to get a full revelation of God in all of His glory. When the great prophet Isaiah saw the Lord high and lifted up and sitting on His throne, he was also immediately aware of his own condition and cried out, "Woe is me for I am undone (destroyed)! Because I am a man of unclean lips and I dwell in the midst of a people of unclean lips." After his deep repentance and the forgiveness he received (symbolized by the purging of his lips with the coal from the alter), Isaiah was fully surrendered to the Lord and was eager to do whatever would please God. He quickly volunteered for a very difficult assignment to reprove and rebuke people who didn't want to hear until they hardened their hearts and judgment would come. Still he was used to save a remnant for the Lord.

Is. 6

Many others throughout scripture had this same experience of seeing the Lord in His glory, as well as the human condition, before they would be mightily used. Moses had the burning bush encounter and then was declared to be the meekest man on the earth. Paul had met God on Damascus road, and then boasted that he was the chief of sinners who had been saved and called by God's amazing grace. Joshua was fully humbled when he met the Lord of hosts on his way to the Promised Land, and after challenging the people to commitment, boldly and confidently stated, "As for me and my house, we will serve the Lord."

Throughout the Bible this same principle holds true, and for us to love the Lord as He truly deserves, we must fully understand and remember that "he who is forgiven much, loves much, but he who is forgiven little, loves little." As we think of the magnitude of God's love and forgiveness in the light of who He is and who we are in comparison, may our love for Him not only stay strong, but also continue to grow deeper. If our love begins to weaken and grow cold, may He give us a new revelation both of Himself and of who we are without Him, so that we never take His love for granted.

17

How Much Love Does The Lord Expect?

There are many people in our society and sitting in our churches who do not really understand the story of the Pharisee and the sinful woman, or the message it portrays. When they read such an account, they are likely to agree with Simon, that such an emotional display is quite crude and certainly too extreme to be considered spiritual. Our reaction to this type of uncontrolled outburst would probably be more of pity or even disgust, rather than envy or rejoicing. It's just not proper, acceptable religious activity and should not be tolerated by any respected man of God.

And what about the incredible waste of pouring the expensive oil on Jesus' feet? Like Judas, when Mary also performed such an extravagant act of devotion, we probably would be thinking of all the practical ways the money could be used. Surely Jesus should at least rebuke this woman for her actions even if He made allowance for her extreme emotionalism. Imagine Simon's shock when Jesus actually commended her behavior and held it up as an example of the kind of love He is looking for.

Jn. 12:5

Does Jesus really want us to get carried away like this woman in expressing our love to Him? Isn't it enough that I put Him first in my life, that I go to church regularly, and that I put my offering in the collection plate? I even occasionally go to special meetings and sow into special offerings for the needy. How much love does the Lord expect?

Jesus makes that abundantly clear when he says, "He who loves father, mother, son or daughter more than me is not worthy of me..." By this statement He is letting us know that our devotion to Him should be greater than our commitment to even our closest human relationships. In fact we must love Jesus so much more than anyone or anything, including our own life, that we are willing to lose everything for His sake.

Mt. 10:37

Paul strongly states this truth in his letter to the Philippians, "What things were gain to me, those things I have counted as loss...Moreover, I have counted all things loss for the surpassing worth of knowing Christ Jesus my Lord, for whom I have suffered the loss of all things and count them as garbage (dung) that I may gain Christ..." He was making it clear to them and to us today, that knowing Jesus in a deep, intimate and personal way, was far more important and satisfying than anything the world has to offer.

Lk. 14:26

Phil. 3:7-8

Jesus explains this truth in Luke when He says that to be His disciple our love for Him must be so great that our love for anyone else, or even our own life, seems like hate in comparison. Doesn't that sound pretty extreme? Surely Jesus wouldn't expect us to love Him in such a radical way.

Probably the best way to think about the kind of love the Lord desires is in relation to our marriages. When I remember the days that my wife Susan and I first met, I can't help but smile. We thought about each other all the time and wanted to spend as much time together as we could. Even though we lived a distance apart, we stayed close by writing and talking on the phone on a regular basis. While we both had busy lives, nothing else seemed to matter as much as communicating or just being together. More and more we began to look forward to the day when we could be together for the rest of our lives and share our love more fully. We were very jealous for each other's commitment in time, energy and affection. Neither of us would have been happy with or settled for the crumbs or leftovers.

Do you think Sue would have been impressed if I would have said, "You're definitely the most important person in my life, and I promise to give you at least five more minutes each week than any of the other women I know or the guys I hang around with. I will also try to occasionally make an effort and even spend a little money if necessary to keep you happy while I pursue my work and recreation interests." For some women that might be an improvement from their present circumstance, but I know that Sue would not have been pleased nor would she put up with that attitude today.

My wife wants to know that she is way more important than anyone or anything else in my life (other than God!), and she is not afraid to let me know it. In fact, she is very good about telling me her desires and making suggestions about ways that I can satisfy her needs! I asked her to do that when we were preparing to get married because I knew that I was not particularly sensitive in that way and wanted to be a good husband. I also asked her to keep reminding me, since I often am forgetful, until I get in the habit (though I did hope she would not do it in a negative or nagging way!). Also, I even suggested she get specific because I don't always pick up on hints or suggestions.

Much of what I'm sharing here in my relationship with my wife is very much the same as God's heart toward us. He wants to be first in our lives by a long way, not slightly ahead of other people or things. The scripture states that He yearns jealously for His people and considers it adultery when we allow other things to take His place in our hearts! There are many warnings both to Israel and the church about the dangers of setting our affections on the things of this world rather than being wholehearted lovers of God.

James 4:4-5

The Bible is both a love story to us and a manual for cultivating our love and commitment to Him. Throughout the history of God's dealing with man, He profoundly declares and demonstrates His amazing love for us. He also makes it very clear about the kind of love He desires and expects from us, as well as shows how such a love can be developed. It starts by fully realizing and then remembering who He is, who we are compared to Him, and the magnitude of His mercy and grace in seeking to bring us into a close relationship with Him. Our recognition and acceptance of His invitation always leads to the next step, which is repentance.

18

Forgetting What Lies Behind

Cultivating our love for Jesus begins with our willingness to really see Him for who He is and letting go of what we want Him to be. Too often we have tried to make God into our image so that we can get what we want instead of acknowledging that we were created in His image for His purpose and glory. True repentance, then, is mainly about confessing and turning away from our false gods and our attempts to create our own life and salvation. Only then can we receive the One True God and the life, love and salvation that He has for us.

Chasing after things other than God comes from a variety of reasons and they can be placed into four categories: selfishness, pride, ignorance and fear. The last two are largely due to the work of the devil who constantly seeks to deceive and destroy our faith. When we truly see the Lord for who He is and trust in His love and truth, these doors that the enemy has so often used against us, begin to close. However, because our old nature wants to regain control, selfishness and pride remain a continuous threat to our walk with God and our growth in love.

That is why Jesus very boldly and clearly declares that the conditions of true discipleship to be: "… deny yourself and take up your cross daily." We need to be constant and progressive about denying our selfish desires, so that we, (like Paul) can die daily to our rights and ambitions – only then can we truly follow our Master on the path of life and love. For this to happen we must be willing to make repentance a regular part of our lifestyle. As we acknowledge,

Lk. 9:23

confess, and forsake our self-sufficiency, and our frequent attempts to construct our own life and salvation, we can allow the Spirit to fill us with God's abundant life and perfect love. Of course we must first listen to the Spirit's voice of conviction who gently reminds us when we have begun to stray from God's path, "No, this is the way. Walk in it."

If we are going to follow Jesus and love Him as He desires and deserves, then we must first be willing to turn away from everything else that once captured our hearts. In order to go forward, it is necessary to leave the past behind, both the good and the bad, and not even look back. Jesus said that "a man who puts his hand to the plow and then looks back is not fit for the Kingdom of God." How can we walk a straight path with and to Jesus when we're always looking back to our past blessings or looking around for a better deal? Remember Lot's wife who longingly looked back to her prosperity and it hardened her to God's future purposes.

Lk. 14:33

There are many people today who claim to be Christians but have never fully given their heart to Jesus because of the things in their life that they were not willing to give up. How can we fully receive Jesus and the love He has for us if we are firmly hanging onto other people or things? Unless we are willing to let go and open our heart to Him, we will never fully know Him and we will be in constant danger of being pulled away from Him altogether. That is why Jesus commanded us to love Him way more than we love anyone else and said that we could not be His follower if we would not "give up all that we have."

Phil. 3:13-14

This verse is also a great reminder to those of us who have made a sincere commitment to Christ not to allow other interests to creep back in and take His place in our life. He wants to be and must be our highest priority if we are going to be prepared for His coming or even make it to the end. That means not only letting go and giving up the things of the past that we once thought were so important, but we must also "forget those things that are behind and strain forward to the things ahead in order to press toward the goal of the prize of the upward call of God in Christ Jesus."

While we know this is true of negative things, such as our hurts and mistakes, it is often difficult to fully release them and they become like a chain that binds us to the past. Unless that chain is broken, we are like the dog that runs toward the promise only to get stopped short and be jerked back. The only way to get free from both the sin we have committed, and the sin committed against us is through the blood of Jesus, which comes through giving and receiving forgiveness. True forgiveness includes the necessity of forgetting.

When we sin against God and/or others, we must be quick to confess as soon as we realize it, through the conviction of the Holy Spirit. I always ask the Lord to forgive and also to cleanse me form all unrighteousness. In that way, I am seeking not only to have my sin covered by the blood, but to have both the memory and desire removed from me, so that I will not continue to repeat it. Like David, my sincere desire is for the Lord to "create in me a clean heart and renew a steadfast sprit within me," which is more than just an outward purging and washing. That is why David was called a man after God's heart, because in spite of his many and major shortcomings, he didn't want to lose the presence of the Lord.

I Jn. 1:9
Ps. 51:10

In the same way, when others sin against us, we must be quick not only to forgive, but to also apply the blood of Jesus to cleanse us from the hurtful grip of the memory of that sin. Since true forgiveness also means forgetting and wiping the slate clean, it is a lie to say, "I have forgiven him, but I will never forget what he did to me!" While it's true that the enemy may bring back the memory, those who have truly forgiven (which often takes time, prayer and faith) will not feel the emotional pain of it as before. There is a peace and freedom in Christ that allows us to go forward into all He has for us.

I Jn. 1:7

Finally, we must be willing to let go and leave behind even the good things of the past in order to go forward into the better and best that God has for us. This is often the most difficult part because many of the things we once thought were so important to us, were not sinful in themselves. Because they felt and seemed "good" parts of our previous life, it is hard to understand why Jesus would want us to give them up. Doesn't He want us to be happy? Wouldn't all these things fit nicely into whatever else He has for us?

Often we were very committed to these things, believing they were the most pleasurable and meaningful parts of a life, that is so often painful and without purpose. It's almost frightening to conceive of life without them. In many ways it would be like saying good-bye to our best friends. No wonder we tend to cling so tightly to them or at least to the memory, thinking we can always go back if this adventure with Jesus doesn't work out.

Therein lies the danger and is the reason we must not only leave our past behind, but also forget what lies behind, in order to truly follow Jesus Christ. Like Paul, we must count as loss and be willing to suffer the loss of everything we once thought was gain, seeing everything else as garbage or dung compared to gaining and knowing Jesus in a deep personal way. We must see Him as being of far surpassing worth like the pearl of great price and the treasure hidden in a field, who is worth us selling everything, in order to receive the King and His Kingdom. Jesus certainly gave His all for us, as well as secured the Kingdom for us (which is the alternative interpretation of these parables).

Phil. 3:8
Mt. 13:44-46

In other words we must be careful to hold everything and everyone in our life loosely as we cling to and press into our relationship with Jesus Christ. Above all, it is necessary to guard our hearts so that nothing, or no one else, takes Jesus' rightful place, when is the highest place, far above all else.

19

Put Away Your Idols

One of the most popular television programs in recent years is called "American Idol," which draws millions of viewers to vote for their favorite singer/performer. Eventually it is narrowed down to one person who is declared to be the American idol for that year. During the process a number of the contestants begin to attract a large group of devoted followers and many of them go on to become stars who receive a great deal of fame and wealth. While it is certainly an entertaining show, I can't help but wonder if there isn't a larger message behind it that we need to recognize.

The truth is there are many idols in America that can boast of millions of devoted followers. I'm sure it would be an exciting and a great competition to see which would be voted #1. However, while it may be entertaining, perhaps we would be missing the real point. Regardless of which would receive highest honors, the fact remains that all of them might take a higher place than God in our lives and become an object of worship.

This is the true meaning of the word "idol." Every person who claims to be a Christian and wants to be ready for Jesus' return should honestly and carefully examine their own hearts. It's very easy to see the idols in the world around us, but often we overlook those within. As I thoroughly scrutinize my life, especially where I put my time, money and effort, I will have discovered my true priorities and whether I have placed anything or anyone else above God.

If we are going to get back to the deep love we had when we first gave our hearts to Jesus, certainly we would need to repent and turn away from anything that has become an idol to us. This can be everything, even good things such as a spouse, children, a hobby, work, recreation, religion, etc., when we allow it to capture our hearts and take a higher place than God. Whatever we begin to look to for life and salvation from the boredom and pain we experience, may become our god and we will begin to set up our altars of worship. While it may not be deliberate or even fully recognized, it is obvious to God and most of the people around us where our affections truly are focused. We may say we love God, but our actions speak louder than words. (My wife likes to hear me say, "I love you!" but if the words are not backed up by specific actions, they will eventually become hollow and meaningless.)

There are many strong warnings in the Bible that speak of the dangers of allowing our hearts to be drawn away from God. Throughout the Old Testament we read of the Israelites hanging onto and continually turning back to the idols of Egypt, the gods of the past. Since every idol in Egypt was thought to be in control of one of their material needs, it was obvious that they didn't fully trust in God's love or in His ability to provide. No matter how many times He miraculously delivered them or abundantly supplied their needs, as soon as the next problem arose they were ready to stone Moses and go back to Egypt. Consequently, only Caleb and Joshua, men of faith who were fully devoted to God and His purposes, made it into the Promised Land. Let that be a warning to us!

In God's eyes hanging onto the gods of the past is like a man who stays in touch and seeks to maintain a relationship with his old girlfriends in case it doesn't go well with his marriage. What do you think will happen as soon as the honeymoon is over and the inevitable problems begin to arise? The Word teaches that our God is very jealous in that, like any of us, He does not want His beloved chasing after or having affairs with others. He declares it to be spiritual adultery, and while He loves us enough to receive us again if we truly repent and turn back to Him, He eventually deals very severely with covenant breakers. The Lord is a very committed, covenant keeping God and He expects us to be as well.

That is why we are commanded to put away our idols, which means to forcefully cast them far away from our lives so we won't be tempted to go back when things get tough. With God's help we can burn our idols, those bridges to the past, so that we can forget what lies behind and press forward to the fullness of our relationship with Him and His purposes for us.

However, even if we have managed to make a clean break from our past idols, there will be plenty more along the way, seeking our attention and affection. As we walk with the Lord, we must be careful to only have eyes for Him, to fix our eyes on Jesus and set our hearts on the things above. Those who have wandering eyes, who are always looking for the better deal, will have many temptations to be drawn away by the gods of this present world. In his continual and determined effort to turn us away from Jesus, the enemy will come up with many new creative ways to capture our hearts.

It doesn't take a prophet or Bible scholar to tell us that our society is full of idols begging for our attention and devotion. At the very time when the bride should be making herself ready, we find many believers falling away from their love for Christ. While the early church saw people added daily because of their devotion to Jesus and His ways, the church today is experiencing frequent subtraction as people drift away, distracted and chasing after other lovers.

Could it be that Satan knows even more than we do that the time is getting close for the Lord's return? As knowledge increases through the internet and other forms of technology, the world is being flooded with evil and constant distractions from the one thing needed: the knowledge of God. More and more we have lost the simplicity of Christ – that He is our all in all and in Him are hidden all the treasures of wisdom and knowledge. In our lust for pleasure and power we are losing sight of all that we were created and redeemed for – to glorify God and enjoy Him forever.

At the very time when we should be deeply in love with Jesus and anxiously awaiting His return and our wedding day, many have allowed their love for Him to grow cold and have instead gone after other gods. God clearly warns us in His Word that many will be deceived and fall away, many will have their love for God grow lukewarm and even cold, and many will allow their hearts to be captured by idols. Who has heeded his warning? Jesus commanded His disciples to watch, pray and be ready for His coming, but many are asleep or caught up in the world and the things of this world.

Rather than seeking God and living to please Him, a great number even in the church are living to please themselves and are only looking to

Him for what they can get. It's definitely time to put away our idols and begin to turn our hearts back to Him before its too late. First, we must be willing to recognize and acknowledge the many things that have drawn our affections away from God.

20

Do Not Love the World or the Things of the World

We have become such a wealthy and prosperous nation that materialism, or the god of mammon, has become a major distraction for the people of God. So many are looking to money and all that it can buy as the way to a good life. Those who have money are rarely satisfied and continually looking for ways to get more. Those of us who have very little spend much of our time wishing we had more and searching for ways to obtain it. Whether we have lots or little, the desire for and pursuit of money can easily become our main focus.

Some are seeking wealth for the power and prestige it can bring, believing this will make them feel important. Others only want to fill up their lives with possessions hoping it will somehow bring a sense of satisfaction. Whatever the reason, many in our society have fallen for the deception that money and possessions are the answer to the longing in our hearts. If only we would listen to the testimony of Solomon who had everything the world could offer and declared it to be vanity, futility, and emptiness – like chasing after the wind.

Before I go further I want to make it clear that I do not think it is necessarily evil or wrong to have money or material possessions. I believe God wants to bless his children, and money can be a valuable tool to advance the Kingdom. However, we must always guard our hearts and examine our motives to make

I Tim. 6:10

sure that we hold it all loosely, so that our money and things do not have us! While money in itself is not evil, the scripture is clear that "the love of money is the root of all kinds of evil" and that it has caused some to "stray from the faith in their greediness and pierce themselves through with many sorrows."

The current mortgage/banking crisis perfectly illustrates this truth. Seeking to capitalize on the greed of the American consumer (who want it all and want it now!), many banks made loans readily available that were at or exceeding the limit of people's ability to repay. As soon as the economy began to turn downward, the snowball gathered speed toward foreclosures then personal and corporate bankruptcy. With the individual and national debt at an all time high we now stand on the brink of the greatest financial crises since the Great Depression. So, our government seeks to hold off disaster by lending billions of dollars we don't have, which greatly increases our national debt, in hopes that it will once again increase consumer confidence to borrow and spend money we don't have. Where does it end?

Col. 3:5
I Jn. 2:14

There is much talk from our economic and political leaders who are trying desperately to come up with this financial bailout in order to prevent a collapse similar to the great depression. Rather than seeking to hold things together with band aids and mirrors, maybe it's time to get down to the real issues. It should be obvious that the problems we are facing in our nation and the world have to do with the condition of our hearts. Selfishness and greed or covetous (which is idolatry!) have turned our hearts away from God to the things of this world. Maybe the crisis we are coming to is God's way of calling us back to Himself...

The apostle John, the beloved friend of Jesus, warned us, "Do not love the world or the things in the world. If anyone loves the world, the love of the Father is not in him." He further explains that the world system is full of "the lust of the flesh, the lust of the yes, and the pride of life", which is certainly not of the Father. Why would we set our hearts on things that are temporary and passing away rather than loving God and seeking to do what pleases Him forever? One reason is that we often seek instant gratification rather than lasting but delayed rewards. Like Esau, we too might be tempted to sell our birthright – all the promises, provisions and power of the Kingdom – for some immediate worldly satisfaction.

It's not that we just totally turn our back on God and head off to seek our fame and fortune (like the prodigal son). At least in the beginning, we become convinced through our own rationalizations spurred on by the enemy of our soul, that we can serve God and still have all the best the world has to offer. Jesus made it clear that such an approach would not work when he said, "No one can serve two masters; for either he will hate on and love the other, or else be loyal to the one and despise the other. You cannot serve God and mammon" (riches, money, materialism). God wants our undivided love and devotion and knows that those who seek other lovers are fickle and will soon walk away from Him.

The devil understands this truth better than we do and has often used it against the people of God. In His message to the church at Pergamos Jesus calls this device of Satan the "doctrine of Balaam." When he couldn't earn his reward by cursing the Israelites because of their obedience and God's protection, Balaam taught king Balak how to defeat Israel by getting them to compromise. They offered to give them the best of their nation which led to sexual immorality and idol worship, further leading to God's judgment. It worked so well that the enemy continues to use this same tactic today with even greater results.

Rev. 2:14

This subtle tactic against God's people has even infiltrated the church in America. In an effort to gather large crowds many have watered down the gospel message to appeal to the modern mindset. The focus in these places is on all that God wants to do for you, the great promises and blessings He desires to give His children so that you can have your "best life now". There is little or no mention of the discipline, responsibility and sacrifice required of a true follower of Christ since that could be offensive and could cause them to seek another church with a message they want to hear. Consequently, many of our churches in America are filled with casual attendees instead of true disciples or as some have aptly called it, they are a mile wide and an inch deep.

Rather than preaching and modeling the full gospel of the Kingdom in order to transform our world (like the early disciples who were accused of turning the world upside down) we have sought to fit in, to adopt a worldly mindset and methods. Consequently it is now very hard to distinguish between the average church goer and the person on the street. Instead of the church invading and changing every aspect of our society, the world has come in and settled down in the church. We then decided the world didn't look too bad and in fact might offer many benefits. So why not make friends?

The apostle James makes it very clear that friendship with the world is far worse than just being a bad idea. In fact he calls it adultery which implies infidelity, unfaithfulness and breaking vows to love and serve the Lord. He even goes on to say that those who turn their hearts to worldliness and materialism have becomes estranged and makes himself an enemy of God. Doesn't that describe quite accurately the condition of this nation and much of the church today and could this be another sign of the end times?

Jms. 4:4

21

Get Rid of the Last Days Lovers

In the book of II Timothy, Paul shares some of the conditions we will see on the earth in the last days before Jesus returns to finally and fully establish His Kingdom. He states that "perilous times will come" (very hard, difficult, stressful, dangerous, etc.) because of the condition of men's hearts. Paul is speaking here of so called Christian who have a form of religion but have denied its power, which comes from the Spirit through a personal relationship with Christ. Rather than loving God they have become lovers of themselves, lovers of money and pleasure, which deteriorates into all kinds of evil, violence and self-centered behaviors. Can anyone deny that this is exactly the condition of America at this time?

II Tim. 3:1-5

We must repent for all the things we have allowed to take God's place in our lives, most of which fit into one of these categories – lovers of self, money and/or pleasure. It always starts with putting our own interests ahead of honoring and pleasing the Lord! So much of our society today directs us toward the philosophy that "it's all about me." Humanism has become the major religion in America, thanks to the main anti-Christian doctrine of evolution, man has become his own god since he is the highest evolved species. Refusing to acknowledge and submit to the one true God, we have chosen instead to construct our own religion. Thus, we see the relative truth and moral relativity of our post-modern world where there are no absolutes and each person decides what's best for himself.

Even the church is full of the humanistic mindset. These are people who believe in God but only that He exists for them. In other words, God is here to make me happy and God sent Jesus for my happiness and Jesus died so that I can be happy forever. Since I am the center of my world and God wants me to be happy, I am free to pick and choose whatever parts of the Bible that fit my desires and agenda. If I want something and it feels good to me, then certainly God would not withhold any pleasure from His child.

That we have devolved into a pleasure seeking society is hardly debatable. For many years our culture has been inundated through the media with the philosophy: "If it feels good, do it" and "How can this be wrong when it feels so right?." Rather than loving God and trusting that His will is best and His way is right, we have become those whom Paul calls the "enemies of the cross of Christ." He goes on to describe these people with his heart breaking as those "whose god is their belly, who set their mind on earthly things, whose glory is their shame and their end is destruction."

Phil. 3:18-19

Shouldn't that be a warning to a nation that has pulled out all the stops in order to satisfy the flesh? Our love of money is largely a means to fulfill the lust for selfish pleasure, which has become increasingly more costly in every meaning of the word. When you look at the amount of time and money spent in this nation on entertainment, recreation and feeding our appetites, it's impossible to deny that we have become lovers of pleasure rather than lovers of God. The time the average person wastes just watching television, movies, video games and/or computer screens is staggering! It is obvious that the enemy of our soul has used the world's technology to hook into our flesh and draw us away from God.

Repent, therefore and return to the Lord and He will return to you. If the Lord is coming soon, we must be willing to do whatever it takes to prepare ourselves. For those who have become very committed and attached to other lovers, it may require drastic measures, but our reward is definitely worth every effort and sacrifice. Jesus told His disciples, "If your eye causes you to sin, pluck it out and cast it from you. And if your hand causes you to sin, cut if off and cast it from you. It is more profitable for you to have one of your members perish than for your whole body to be cast into hell."

To most Christian that may seem extreme, but not when you consider the alternative and realize that hell is a horrible place! Maybe we could start by throwing away our mouse and remote control, and if that doesn't work, we could get rid of the computer and television. That would at least show the Lord we mean business, and it would get us started on the process of removing the idols of the world from our lives so that God could once again have His rightful place. We must begin to recognize how far away we've gotten from the love we once had for Jesus, and do all we can to stir up the passion.

It is important to remember that it is not enough to clean out the idols from our hearts and lives, to get rid of all our other lovers. If the enemy comes back and sees the house swept clean, he may return with other help that would cause us to fall farther away from God than before. After we repent for our idol worship and ask God to help us cleanse the temple, it is necessary to return to the first works – to fill our lives with the things of God. Whatever draws us closer to Jesus and strengthens our love for Him, we must pursue with all of our hearts.

22

It is Time to Wake Up!

As we stand on the very edge of the Lord's return, all of God's people should be in a constant state of alert fulfilling His commands to watch, pray and be ready. However, like the early disciples who were asked to pray with Him at a very critical hour, I'm afraid He will find many asleep, especially in the American church. Instead of looking and longing for His coming, we find ourselves in a state of slumber, hypnotized by the enemy who has constantly waved the world in front of our eyes. Though the signs of the last days are all around us and increasing, most people seem to be in a state of denial or oblivious to the things that are coming upon us.

We would do well to heed Paul's warning to the Roman church when he declared it to be a kairos hour, a key time of crisis and challenge. In the light of the Lord's soon and sudden return, he urged them, "it is high time to awake out of sleep; for our salvation is nearer than when we first believed." He went on to declare that "the day is at hand" and reminded them of the importance of being ready. To help us wake up, God Himself is shaking everything that can be shaken to try to get our attention. He is no longer whispering but shouting for His people to arise and prepare for His coming.

Rom. 13:11-14

Our preparedness requires immediate and diligent effort both in a negative and in positive direction. First, Paul challenges us to "cast off the works of darkness" and "make no provision for the flesh." His meaning is clear: in light of the Lord's soon return throw off those things of the old, selfish nature and stop making plans to gratify our carnal desires. Throw it as far from you as you can with the Spirit's help and don't even think about reeling it back in! It is time to stop pampering and making excuses for the flesh and begin to see it as our mortal enemy.

In Galatians Paul describes a war going on inside of us between the flesh and the Spirit, which most Christians would be quick to acknowledge.

Gal. 5:17

One is pulling us toward our own pleasure and satisfaction while the other seeks to pull us toward pleasing God by obeying His will for our lives. This tug of war for control of our lives continues until one gains the upper hand and we begin to move steadily in one direction or the other. Perhaps the most exciting and frightening part of this final outcome is that we have the deciding vote!

We have been given a free will so that we can choose to love and obey God, which also requires us to "deny our self and take up our cross daily" in order to follow Jesus. This means we must die daily to our selfish ways or as Paul say "by the Spirit you put to death the deeds of the body (mortify the flesh!)" He makes it clear that the flesh is not your friend and those who live by it will be on a path of destruction and death. It is crucial to understand that the flesh is our enemy and the door through which our other enemies – the world and the devil – can get their hook in us. We must kill the flesh before it kills us!

The preferred method of dealing with the flesh presented in scripture (before we get to the point of needing to pluck out our eye or cut off our hand!) is to starve it. This leads us to one of the most neglected spiritual

Rm. 8:13

disciplines – fasting – which was meant to be a regular part of the Christian lifestyle. Jesus modeled this life of prayer and fasting, and even declared that some spiritual victories can only be won through this powerful combination. However, for most believers in our soft society, "fast" is another "four letter word," (like work!) and is reserved for special occasions that of course never come. Consequently, most American Christians would admit that the flesh has gained the upper hand in the inner battle, and we are too often driven and ruled by the lower nature and desires.

It is definitely time to wake up from the delusion of our own excuses and rationalizations and begin to seriously deal with our flesh, or risk being unprepared for the Lord's coming. In our so-called advanced society and mindset, there are plenty of "good" reasons to indulge the flesh. Only those who truly love the Lord and want to please Him above all else, will have the discipline and determination (though prayer and the power of the Spirit) to resist the flood of temptation and take their stand in and for the Lord.

Paul unequivocally states that "those who are in the flesh cannot please God." In the preceding chapter he has very accurately described the struggle between the flesh and the Spirit, stating that he often does the very thing he hates, rather than the good that he wants to do. He also acknowledges that it is not within his own effort and ability that he is able to overcome this tendency, but knows as Jesus stated to his disciples, "the spirit is willing but the flesh is weak." Only by the blood of Jesus and the power of the Holy Spirit can we be set free from the "law of sin and death." You can't fight the flesh by the flesh(willpower) but only through His power.

Rom. 8:8

If you are wondering how you are actually doing in your war against the flesh, Paul lists some of the works of the flesh in Galatians 5:19-21. This is not a complete list but most of us can probably see a few areas that we need to examine more carefully and perhaps deal with more firmly. It should give us all the incentive we need when he closes the section by boldly declaring that those who practice such things will not inherit the kingdom of God. While he is talking here about those who make a habit of such behavior rather than the occasional slip up, it is certainly a warning about the danger of allowing our flesh to gain a measure of control. There is potential for it to take us away from God to the point where, like Samson, Esau or Judas, we may find it hard to get back.

As we begin to wake up out of our deception and complacency, it is essential for us to throw off the blankets of comfort and convenience. In order to run the race with endurance so that we make it all the way to the end, we must be willing to "lay aside every weight and the sin which so easily ensnares us." Then we must "fix our eyes on Jesus," which implies looking at Him with undivided attention and looking away from all distractions. This will continually give us the faith and courage to finish our race as we keep our eyes on the true prize.

While it starts by repenting and turning back to God, we must continued to walk with Him and even run as we see this race coming to the end. That means we must be willing to throw off anything that hinders our progress, which includes not only the present distractions but the bondage of the past. Jesus revealed this truth when after raising Lazarus from the dead, He turned to those around Him and said, "Loose him, and let him go." Part of the work of the church, once a person has been born again into the

Heb. 12:12

family of God, is to help them untie and unwrap the grave clothes that we were bound with when we were dead in our trespasses and sin.

So many in the church today make little or no progress in the faith because they are caught in time, stuck in the place where they received a deep wound. This keeps their focus on themselves and their circumstances rather than Jesus, and instead of pressing into their healing, they remain in fear and/or self-pity. Could it also be due to the fact that few people in the church have been willing and/or capable to step into this difficult place and offer to release the healing of Jesus to those with broken hearts? It may take a commitment of time and effort to help them get free of their grave clothes so that they can more fully run the race with Christ.

How can we go forward unless we deal with both the bondage of the past and the present temptations of the flesh, both of which could weigh us down or trip us up? Those who are wholehearted lovers of God and want to please and honor Him will do all they can with the help of the Holy Spirit to lay hold of the fullness of the great salvation, freedom and victory that Jesus has purchased with such a high price. I don't want Him to have suffered in vain for any aspect of my life, and I want to fully glorify and reveal Him to everyone that He puts in my path. The more I am cleansed, the more I can be filled with Him. I must decrease so that He can increase in and through my life. As I am filled with Him and changed from glory to glory into His likeness, I will more fully honor Him and represent Him to others – a true Ambassador of Christ.

23

Be Filled with the Fullness of God

God's purpose for each of us is that we would enjoy His fellowship and reveal His love and glory. As we continue to make room and open our hearts and lives to Jesus, He will fill us up to overflowing so that out of our innermost being will flow rivers of living water to everyone God puts in our path. It is possible to be so full of God that we couldn't contain it even if we wanted to (why would we want to keep it to ourselves?). Wouldn't you like to be anointed to the bone like Elisha, whose bones caused a dead man to come alive when he was put into his grave? Or how about the early disciples who released healing when they sent a handkerchief or when their shadow fell on people as they were walking by?

II Kings 13:21

The truth is that we are going to be filled with something. God created us in His image (even though we fell and His glory in us was marred by sin), and there is a longing for our original condition, since He places a sense of eternity in our hearts. I can remember the early days to the hippie movement in the 1960's and 70's when many young people were searching for something to fill the void within. We had already rejected the dead religious formalism found in many churches at the time, and we were equally turned off by the middle class alternative – a job in the corporate world, a nice house in the suburbs with two cars in the garage, two children, a color T.V., boat and snowmobile.

While it's true that many were simply in rebellion against authority and the status quo, there were some of us who sensed that there had to be something greater than we were being offered. Unfortunately, with the help of Satan and the music that he inspired at the time, many began to experiment with mind altering drugs and Eastern religions. We somehow knew that what we were seeking was a spiritual experience with God, and the devil was faithful to help us find everything but Jesus. Of course many of us had already rejected Him based on our experience with the church, which seemed to offer only rules, ritual and hypocrisy. And since it is impossible to find the way without the One who is the way, many of that generation remained lost and some crashed and burned on the choices they made.

I am still amazed and so very thankful that I was one who not only survived that destructive time, (though not without scars and painful memories!) but who finally came back around full circle to find Jesus. At least we told others that we had found Jesus, but He wasn't the one who was lost! Actually it was more like after searching in all the wrong places and refusing to look His way, He knocked me down and put His foot on my neck and then I said, "I found Jesus!" Anyway, I am so thankful He finally got my attention, even if it was through a very devastating time of crushing. Now looking back I can say He is everything I was looking for and much, much more.

It was evident to everyone who knew me that a true conversion had taken place. While the fullness of His work in me is ongoing, from that point in my life I began moving in a whole new direction. Realizing finally that Jesus was what my heart had been longing for in all my years of searching, I found that I couldn't get enough of Him or His Word. I wanted to know Him and His will for my life and I diligently pressed into anything that might help me draw closer to God and walk in His ways.

In those days my constant prayer was derrived from Paul's letter to the church of Ephesus. My deepest desire was that God would strengthen me by His Spirit to go forward in order to receive more of Christ and His amazing love. It seemed incredible that I could actually "be filled with all the fullness of God", but at least I knew that I wanted everything He had for me so that I could be all He wanted me to be. The next verse has always been my source of faith and motivation to keep going on no matter how difficult it gets or how strong the tendency to be satisfied with what I've already

Eph. 3:16-19

received. I keep reminding myself that God has more that He wants to do in and through my life. In fact, it is way more than I could ask or even imagine because of the power of His Spirit working in me to bring glory to His name.

Why would we want to settle for so little when God wants to give us so much and work through us in awesome ways to display His mighty power and glory?! Perhaps we have forgotten that it's all about Him and all for His glory, rather than our happiness. Those who truly love Him will want to do anything and everything that will please Him and bring honor to His name. The more we spend time with Him, the more we receive of and from him, and the more we can bear fruit to glorify Him.

This was a truth I learned early in my walk with the Lord, and so I began to look for opportunities to draw close to Him and learn His ways. I didn't have to try to give up the many things that had drawn my heart away from God. He became much more important and real to me, and my love for Him was so overwhelming that He was the focus of my attention. In the light of His amazing love and glory everything else fell away, and all I desired or could think of was pressing into Him and His plan for my life. My relationship with Jesus was so awesome to me that He was always on my mind and the first thing I wanted to talk about. Because of this, many others came to know and believe in Him, including all of my family! Those were amazing days filled with love and grace!

Unfortunately, this initial excitement eventually began to grow cold from religious routine and was crowded out from much religious activity. Like so many others, I allowed my love relationship to get stale and to take a backseat to busyness. Instead of enjoying and following Jesus, I began to settle for a form of religion, fulfilling my religious duties and obligations. I got so busy doing things for Jesus that I had little time to spend with Him, and so this once vital love affair became only a distant memory. I got so caught up in doing ministry and doing church and doing devotions that I no longer had time to just enjoy Jesus. Now, at a time when I need to be close to Jesus, I was feeling very distant and disconnected, which is neither satisfying nor safe.

That is exactly the reason God is calling us back to our first love. Only those with a deep passion for and commitment to Jesus will be prepared for His coming and for the difficult times which will precede His return. It is our love for Him that will enable us not only to endure to the end, but do all He desires us to do before that great and glorious day. It is so crucial for us at this time to do the works we did at first.

We must stir up and cultivate our love and commitment to Jesus. Only love has the power to hold us through very troubled times and provides the motivation to do all He asks to prepare ourselves and others for His coming.

24

Seek the Lord With All Your Heart

God spoke through Jeremiah to His people while they were in captivity in Babylon, He told them that he had great plans for their future and wanted to give them hope and peace. In spite of their continued disobedience and rebellion toward Him, His love and purposes for them remained unchanged. After a time of judgment and discipline (which is a sign of His love), He promised to draw them back to Himself and the fullness of their inheritance. That promise still remains for us today along with the conditions of its fulfillment. The punishment they had received was intended to restore them to a proper relationship with Him. Now they were being encouraged to call upon Him and pray to Him.

For those who have been estranged from God due to sin and the resulting consequences, He still calls out to us today, "you will seek me and find me, when you search for me with all of your heart." This challenge is meant to draw us back to being wholehearted lovers and seekers of God. After we have dealt with and removed those things in our lives that have turned our hearts away from Him, we must then determine to set our hearts, minds, and affections on Him and His Kingdom. This implies a firm decision to seek Him first, far above and beyond everything and everyone else.

Jer. 29:13
Col. 3:2
Mt. 6:33

This is the reason that so many in our society today turn back from seeking and following Jesus Christ and settle for a form of religion. Many have had their heart captured by the things of this world and are not ready to give them up. Like the rich young ruler, they desire eternal life but are not willing to let go of the riches of this life. Essentially, "they want their cake and to eat it too;" – they want Jesus as long as it doesn't cost them anything, and as long as they can have everything else as well. The sad part is that many churches actually preach this gospel and so, people worship both God and mammon. At least the rich ruler walked away sorrowful knowing that he was not ready to make the commitment required.

God is looking for people who love Him enough to seek Him with their whole heart. He promises that He will be found by those who diligently seek Him, who believe in and desire Him to the point that they pursue Him above all else. There is no such promise for the casual seeker, for those who go to church if they have nothing better to do or those who read the Bible once in a while. As was stated previously, the Lord deserves passion from his Bride and will not settle for a complacent, indifferent church that is just going through the motions out of duty. He has made it clear that He is after our hearts and continues to challenge His people to deeper levels of love and commitment.

It may be surprising who God chooses and draws to Himself in those last days, because God does not judge as man does, on outward appearance. We may be shocked at some of the people who will be brought into the Kingdom before the Lord returns. The Lord sees what's in the heart and will be seeking those who are open and longing to know Him. We may very well see pimps and prostitutes, alcoholics and addicts, even Muslims, Hindus and new agers saved and ushered into the wedding banquet before and perhaps instead of the prideful religious crowd. Judging from the makeup of the early church, we probably should expect something similar. One thing is for sure: "the Lord knows those who are His," those who truly want to know Him and live for Him with all their heart.

This is certainly not the time to be a casual church goer or a Sunday morning Christian, nor would we want to be if we really know who Jesus is. Unless we see Him for the incredible treasure that He is, so that we can declare, "thanks be to God for His indescribable gift," we will continually be in danger of being enticed and drawn away by what seems to be a better deal! Settle it now in your heart that Jesus is the right way, the best way and the only way to find true and lasting love, joy, peace and fulfillment for this life and the next. Realize that He is more precious than gold, silver, diamonds, or other jewels, and He is worthy to be sought with our whole heart. Those who find Him, recognize He is definitely worth losing or giving up everything in order to be His. This is the kind of love Jesus is looking for and will have from the Bride He is returning to claim for His own.

Even now many are hearing His call to "return to the Lord will all your hearts with fasting, with weeping, and with mourning." In true repentance and brokenness they are turning from selfish and worldly pursuits to once again seek the Lord. Rather than seeking His hand for what He can give or do for them, it is important to seek His face and declare that He is all we want and need. I often see II Chronicles 7:14 quoted as a revival promise, and because of the deteriorating spiritual condition in our nation, there has been a movement toward prayer. But how many have come to the place of humility and brokenness? How many have turned from their wicked ways? How many are wholeheartedly seeking God's face rather than what they want Him to do for us?

David, who was declared to be a man after God's heart, expresses his deepest desire and shows why he was so beloved of God and blessed in Psalm 27. We would do well to consider his unwavering commitment to seeking the Lord even in times of great trial and oppression from his enemies. He boldly proclaimed, "One thing I have desired of the Lord, that will I seek: that I may dwell in the house of the Lord all the days of my life, to behold the beauty of the Lord, and to inquire in His temple." Later he says with all sincerity, "When you said 'seek my face,' my heart said to you, 'your face Lord, I will seek'".

> Ps. 27:4
> Ps. 27:8
> Ps. 16:11

If we truly desire to be part of the beloved that the Lord is returning for, we must seriously meditate on these words and diligently follow David's example. Put away your "wish list", all those things you want from God (and have been doing everything you can to get them) and get back to just seeking Him. Have we forgotten that He is all that we need and in fact, is way more than enough? Besides, those who seek God not only get Him, but they will also find the path of true Life. Again, David expresses this truth when he writes, "You will show me the path of life; in Your presence is the fullness of joy; at your right hand are pleasures forevermore."

God is looking for those who want Him, who desire and seek His presence and fellowship far above everything else. For many of us, that means getting back our first love, when the Lord was so amazing and exciting to us that He was all we thought about or talked about. Just spending time with Him was all we wanted and we were always looking for opportunities to enjoy His fellowship. Now, we are so caught up in the busyness of the world and religious activities that we seldom have time to even think about Him and rarely experience His presence. At the very time when we should be drawing closer to the Lord and deepening our love for Him, He has become a distant memory and low priority for many that He has called. Is that the kind of Bride He is looking for? Would you want to marry someone who was distant and seemed indifferent? Maybe that is why many will hear, "Depart from me. I never knew you."

25

Seek the Lord Early, Everywhere and Often (Psalm 63)

While the Lord promises to reward those who diligently seek Him, there is no such promise for the casual seeker. Nothing is more indicative of the spiritual condition of the church and the shallowness of the commitment in the many who call themselves "Christians" than the attendance records. Other than the special occasions like Christmas and Easter, (which allows the C & E Christians to feel good for the year) and the few you can count on to be there, you never know who will be in church from one week to the next.

It's amazing to see how many people consider attending church on Sunday as just one option among many. In other words, they will occasionally make their appearance if they feel like it and nothing better comes along. How it must grieve the heart of God to see so many of His people choosing other options on Sunday morning and throughout the week (often as insignificant as a warm, comfortable bed), instead of making time to spend with Him! The world does all it can to foster this self-centered attitude because it sells products, encouraging people to get what they want without considering what it will cost them in the future. Only recently have we begun to reap the results of this mindset, and still we are expecting someone to bail us out of our foolish financial choices.

Even the church, especially the ones we have so aptly labeled as "seeker sensitive," has played along with and encouraged this attitude by focusing on comfort and convenience, or anything else they think people may want. They preach a "man-centered gospel" trying to attract this modern generation by emphasizing all that God wants to give them and of course throwing in plenty of entertainment, which is the spirit of the world.

By successfully marketing the gospel, many have drawn large crowds which requires them to build large, impressive buildings with plenty of conveniences (coffee shops, snack bars, restaurants, etc) and massive debt. This in turn demands that the church provide the kind of programs and performance that keeps the people long enough to get the facilities paid for as well as add the newest technology and entertainment features to keep up with the world.

Where is God in all of this? Where are those who are simply seeking God (whom Tommy Tenney described as "God Chasers")? It's time for the church to get back to the simplicity of Jesus Christ, to seeking and worshipping God and to loving Him with our whole heart before it's too late. We're following the same path as Europe, where you can find huge ornate cathedrals everywhere that are empty of true worshippers – relegated to tourist attractions, mausoleums of dead religion.

Unless you think I'm picking on one particular style of church or worship, I must assure you that I see this same trend in churches across the board. In general, we decide what we want from God and then come up with a plan of how we can get it. Whether it's following rules and/or rituals, praying the right prayer, singing the right songs, paying our tithes and offerings, doing our time of religious service and duty, or the many other ways we try to earn our desired reward! Like the Pharisees, we're diligently trying to earn our salvation and become proud of our efforts, as well as being critical of all who aren't like us.

So many Christians have fallen into the ditch on either side of the path of life. There are those, like the Corinthian church, seeking and even excelling in the gifts, but who are greatly lacking in love for God or others and have fallen into lawlessness. On the other side are those, like the Galatians, who are seeking the latest teaching or adding beliefs from the past and stubbornly clinging to their doctrines, but who are also lacking in love because they have fallen from grace and are estranged from Christ. Where are those who are simply wholehearted lovers and seekers of God and who are living just to honor and please Him by revealing His love to others?

Again we would do well to turn to the example of David, a man after God's heart, who proclaims both his purpose and plan in Psalm 63. First of all, he has fully settled it in his own heart and mind that God is his God. While most people in America claim to believe in God, many do not really know who God is and fewer still have really submitted and surrendered to His Lordship. James says to these kinds of people that they do well to believe or acknowledge God's existence, but even the demons believe (in that way) and they even go one step further in that they tremble in fear, knowing who He is. James is quick to add that this kind of faith will not save you unless it leads to appropriate actions that show the sincerity of your belief.

James. 2:19, 20
John 4
Ps. 63:8
Ps. 91

David was someone who quickly and fully responded to the Lord because he realized that God was all that he wanted or ever needed. After acknowledging His Lordship, David very candidly shares the deep longing in his heart for God and his determination to seek Him early and often. At this time he was in the wilderness hiding from Absalom and the king/poet draws from the symbolism of a "dry and barren land where there is no water." Anytime we are away from the Lord (as David was away from the temple) there is leanness and longing in our soul that only the Living Water can fully satisfy. David knew that God's covenant of love and mercy was far better than anything this life has to offer, and so he was committed to seeking and praising Him with his whole heart.

By declaring that he would seek God early, David was determined to keep the Lord first and foremost in his heart and mind. This is a sharp contrast to so many Christians today who are too caught up in the cares and concerns of the world and God becomes an afterthought. Other than those occasional drastic situations when we know we need some help and, of course, at church which we have set aside as our "God time," He rarely comes to our mind. No wonder our lives are so filled with weariness, frustration and confusion. How much better to follow David's example (and our Lord's command) by seeking Him first rather than as a last resort.

MT 6:33

Does seeking God early imply that I must become a "morning person" who rises at some ungodly hour to do his devotions every day? Not necessarily, but at least we should be willing to meet with God whenever He desires, or whenever we can find a time without distractions. For me, having a house full of six children, the morning became my quality time where I could have enough quiet moments to really focus on the Lord.

While my wife usually wakes up with a time of prayer, her best time to spend seeking the Lord and reading His Word has been at night when everyone else is in bed! Seeking the Lord early is more of an attitude than a specific part of the day. Is God the first one on your mind when you wake up and do you speak with Him throughout your day, or do you mumble a memorized prayer while you're falling asleep at night?

David not only sought God early, but he also looked for Him everywhere. When he went into the temple, the king actually desired to experience the presence of the Lord and hear His voice rather than simply fulfilling his religious obligation. However, David also realized he could seek the Lord anywhere, even in the midst of a barren wilderness, which was so different from many people then and now who tend to reserve their brief experience with God to the church building. Especially the Western mindset has compartmentalized their religion so that our religious duty and "God time" has become the occasional and/or brief visits to church. I have a strong suspicion that God is neither impressed nor satisfied with that type of arrangement. He is looking and longing for much more from His people, His Bride.

In addition to seeking the Lord early and everywhere, David also sought God often throughout the day and night. He very boldly declared that his soul (his heart, mind, will) followed hard after the Lord, which is the perfect example of a "God chaser." Whether it was the heat of the day or the darkest part of the night, David thought about the Lord and even meditated on Him and His word. No wonder he was beloved of the Lord and is held up as a man after God's heart. Both he and Paul might be saying to us today, "follow me as I follow Christ."

Certainly this generation, who may well be standing on the edge of the Lord's return, should look to those who set their hearts on seeking and serving the Lord. How much better it is to be following their example than someone like Solomon, who set his heart to seek human wisdom, wealth, pleasure, accomplishments and everything else the world has to offer. Are we chasing after God or chasing after the wind? One path leads to full and forever satisfaction while the other brings only emptiness and futility. Even if we manage to get everything we want, "what does it profit a man to gain the whole world and lose his soul?" The only place our heart and life is secure is in the Lord's hands.

Fortunately, there is still a remnant of believers today who have not soiled their garments with the contamination of the world, which is full of toxic waste. Many have heard the Lord's voice calling and are seeking to draw closer to Him, which is essential for our protection (under the shadow of the Almighty) as well as for our preparations (keeping our lamps full of oil) in these last days. These are people who's greatest desire is the Lord Himself and who are diligently seeking Him, rather than His gifts and blessings. They know that in His presence is found the fullness of joy, the path of life, and pleasure forevermore. Is there any doubt that these are the kind of people the Lord is looking for, and will soon come back to receive them to Himself?

26

Worship is the Key

In John 4, while talking with a Samaritan woman at Jacob's well, Jesus gave us another key to the kind of people God is seeking. He plainly informs this woman (and all of us today) that the Father is looking for true worshippers who will worship Him in spirit and in truth. Does that surprise you? Only those who do not really know what it means to be a genuine worshipper would have any doubts about this truth (i.e. why does God care whether or not I sing the two hymns on Sunday?). Hopefully, we understand that true worship means more than singing a couple of hymns or choruses on key. In fact, as the recent song by Matt Redmond so accurately states, it's not a song that God desires but a heart full of worship, full of love and devotion to Him.

When we focus on the outward form rather than the inner attitude, we end up with endless arguments and chosen preferences about music and/or style, which totally miss the point. You see, God has an attitude about worship – He thinks it should be all about Him! It's not about what I enjoy or what I'm comfortable with, but what does He desire and how can I truly show my love for Him? How could we possibly believe that the God who loves variety so much that He made every snowflake and fingerprint different, would require one set pattern of worship. In fact the worship styles are as numerous as the many cultures and individual personalities of the human race, and they are all precious and beautiful to God when the heart of the worshipper is given to Him.

Webster defines worship as "showing intense love and admiration for something or someone; to show religious reverence." Do you see now why God both deserves and desires our worship? He is looking and longing for people who will bow in reverence and honor to Him and surrender their lives in loving devotion to the One who is truly worthy. In Greek the word (proskunes) which is translated as "worship," means "to kiss, like a dog licking his master's hand" in devotion and adoration for the One who cares for him. A true worshipper, therefore, will have both a deep respect and holy fear, while at the same time maintaining an attitude of deep love and surrender.

Like a marriage relationship we must be very careful not to allow our love to grow cold through routine or religious formalism. As we keep our eyes on the object of our worship rather than our form of worship, our love for the Lord and knowledge of Him will continue to be strong and growing. Worship is indeed a major key to drawing and staying close to the Lord. Can you see why it is so important to Him and for us?

No wonder David was called a man after God's heart since he was also an example of a true worshipper. He wrote many of the Psalms as songs of worship to the Lord, and we also know that he was well known for releasing praise through his instrument – the harp. Saul originally called him for his soothing worship music, which brought peace to his troubled soul and at least temporarily chased away the tormenting spirits. David understood that worship brings the Lord's presence and power, which is desirable at all times and essential during troubled times.

For David, worship was a means for ever increasing joy and intimacy with the Lord, an ever widening circle of knowledge and closeness. As he drew near in worship, the Lord responded by also drawing closer to David. This brought a greater knowledge of the Lord and His attributes, which in turn inspired deeper levels of praise and surrender. Like the Songs of Ascent, there is a sense of moving onward and upward to the very heights of Mount Zion, to the throne of God and the very presence of the Lord Almighty. In one Psalm he writes, "Ascribe to the Lord glory and strength. Ascribe to the Lord the glory due His name; Worship the Lord in the beauty of holiness." This shows both a true knowledge of the nature of his God and a holy love and reverence for His name.

Perhaps the best example of how deeply David desired and knew he needed the Lord's presence can be seen in II Samuel 6 when he determined to bring back the ark of God to Jerusalem. Initially he was careless and did not take time to consider the proper way of handling God's presence (perhaps he thought good intentions were enough). This cost the life of one of his men and brought a holy fear into David and all of his people.

Still David could not rest until he had brought back the ark and God's holy presence, so he sought the priests to know the Lord's instructions for carrying the ark. Then they proceeded to bring the ark to Jerusalem with many sacrifices and unrestrained worship. David even took off his kingly garment and humbly worshipped the Lord in reckless abandoned to the delight of God and the disgust of his wife.

The Bible records that David even danced before the Lord with all of his might, which indicates that he held nothing back. When his wife admonishes him for making himself look foolish before the people, he lets her know in no uncertain terms that he was worshipping to celebrate before the Lord. It was to show his desire and thankfulness for the Lord's presence that he was rejoicing and not to impress the people or enjoy a religious experience. In fact, David further declares that he is willing to humble himself and look even more foolish if it will bless the Lord and allow him to draw closer to God. Isn't it also worth noting that the one who despised this kind of unrestrained worship ended her life barren and unfruitful? Doesn't this teach us that it is out of our intimacy with Him that we truly bear much fruit for Him and bring glory to His name?

Ps. 29:1,2
II Sam.6:14

Worship, then is our way to show God how much we love Him and how much he means to us by giving our very best to Him. This means the willingness to give Him what He truly desires from us, which is our whole self – body, soul and spirit. He wants it all, not just an occasional piece of our time, energy, money, affection, etc. God is looking and Jesus is coming for those who have truly surrendered their lives to Him, while many of us are still trying to get by with giving Him the scraps and leftovers.

King David was one who understood that God desires, deserves and demands that His people give Him their best and their all. More than simply worshipping in spirit, God wants our body and soul as well. That is why David literally commanded his soul – "Bless the Lord, O my soul, and all that is within me, bless His holy name." Then he proceeded to remind himself of all the amazing benefits and blessings that God has poured out on His people and to praise Him for His very nature and character. In this way he determined (willed) to engage his mind and stir his emotions to an attitude of praise and worship, knowing there is so much to thank and love God for.

While God certainly does not want our praise to be simply soulish, as some would be quick to suggest, neither is He honored by the heartless worship that is so prevalent in our churches today. To the many people who claim to be His followers, Jesus would probably say, as He did to the Pharisees, "This people honor me with their lips, but their heart is far away from me. In vain do they worship me.." God wants more than outward form or style and He is not impressed with lip service praise. He is looking for people, like David, who express their deep spiritual love and longing for Him through their thoughts and emotions. Hence, the longest book in the Bible is Psalms, which is filled with passionate songs of prayer and praise to the Lord.

Many of those Psalms also contain commands (not suggestions) that require certain actions to express our sincere attitude of love and worship.

Rom. 12:1

As we saw in David's willingness to dance before the Lord unreservedly, he fully understood that God wants our body as well as our soul and spirit. The Word of God calls us to "present your bodies a living and holy sacrifice, acceptable to God, which is your spiritual service of worship." This may mean clapping, shouting, lifting our hands, singing, dancing, playing instruments and other types of exuberant praise. Or it could lead to acts of quiet worship and adoration such as bowing, kneeling, lifting our arms in surrender, sitting or lying prostrate in His presence.

All of these and many other forms of worship and praise are appropriate, Biblically accurate, and will bless the Lord when they come from a sincere heart longing to show love and honor to the One who is worthy (rather than simply going through the ritual motions and fulfilling our religious obligations). It's not about what feels comfortable and correct or which do we prefer, but am I, like David, willing to do whatever the Lord desires to show Him my love and bring His presence closer – even if I look foolish to others? This is not easy, especially for those of us who tend to be self-conscious. It may take some time and effort to become or get back to that place where we are God-conscious, where He is the focus of our attention and affection to the point that we want His presence even if it kills us!

Worship is the key because it draws us into a precious cycle of intimacy – we worship to show our love which brings His presence and makes us love and want to worship Him all the more. The truth is that we were made to worship, since we were made for love and worship is a way to express and grow in love. While worship is a choice, the chances are good that we will worship someone or something, so, the real question and choice is, who or what will we worship? If we are wise and want to be the people Jesus is returning for, we will set our hearts and affections on God and His Kingdom rather than the things of this world. He alone is worthy of our full surrender and worship, and only what's done for Him will last... forever.

27

Rejoice in the Lord Always!

One aspect of worship that is especially important if we are going to get back to our first love and then remain close to the Lord is to do what God commands through Paul in his letter to the Philippians – "Rejoice in the Lord always." Just to make sure we understand the significance of this, Paul adds with strong emphasis, "Again I will say, rejoice!" Why does God emphasize this aspect of worship so much?

Many Christians have never fully realized that we have an enemy who wants nothing more than to "steal, kill and destroy." His determined plan for every child of God is to steal all that God has for them and destroy all He wants to do through them by killing their relationship with Him, which cuts them off from the source of life. Even those who read about this warfare in the Word and have heard it preached, rarely acknowledge the seriousness of it or determine to do anything about it. Yes, the victory has been given to us by Jesus Christ our Lord but not without a fight. Why else would God tell Joshua three times to "be strong and courageous" even though He had already promised him the victory. And why would He say to us to "stand in the power of His might" when we wrestle against the powers of darkness and that those who "endure to the end shall be saved."

Jn. 10:10

For those who still don't get it, I want to try to make it perfectly clear – we have an enemy (Satan, the devil, Lucifer) who hates us because of our relationship with God through Jesus Christ. The only way for Satan to get back at Jesus, who defeated him on the cross and made a public spectacle of him, is to hurt His loved ones. So he has launched an all out assault on our hearts hoping we will become so discouraged, distracted and/or deceived that we will drift and eventually walk away from God. These attacks against God's people will actually intensify in the last days as our enemy rages knowing that his time is short and his destination is certain.

In the book, Waking the Dead, John Eldredge describes this war against us in no uncertain terms. "Your life is the story of a long, brutal assault against your heart by the one who knows you and fears what you could be." Satan hates us but also fears what we can become in Christ as we draw closer to God and receive more of His love, truth and power. Therefore, his attack against us is continuous and brutal as he seeks to hit us at our weakest points and our weakest moments. He then presses in to cut us off from God or wound us so our witness is destroyed. Eldredge adds that unless we interpret everything that happens in our life in light of this spiritual warfare, we will probably misinterpret about 80% of our lives. Often we come to the false conclusion (with the enemy's help through his bombardment of our minds with his lies and accusations) that God is mad at us or that either He doesn't really care about us or won't come through for us. All of these destroy our faith and make us pull away from God.

So, how do we combat this constant assault of the enemy? The Word teaches that we have been given an armor of protection, which we must take up and learn how to use effectively. One of the strongest weapons we have in our arsenal is worship and praise. I don't want to go into great detail at this time (perhaps another book will be written about spiritual warfare), but I do want to go back to the command to "rejoice in the Lord always" and how it applies, especially when we are under attack or in very difficult circumstances.

First of all, when we choose to rejoice in the Lord regardless of our situation or feelings, it lifts our eyes and allows us to rise above as we look to the One who loves us and is Lord over everything. This causes faith to rise up within us as it brings an attitude of praise for all God is and a thankfulness for all He has done. Truly, this is how we learn to "encourage ourselves in the Lord," in the face of the enemy's relentless efforts to bring discouragement. It is a means of restoring our joy in the Lord and we know that "the joy of the Lord is our strength." While discouragement makes us weak and susceptible to the enemy's attacks (especially when he gets us to cooperate by giving in to self-pity!), rejoicing renews our faith and brings the strength to overcome.

Our choice to rejoice (isn't that a catchy phrase?!) then, changes us even though it may not change our circumstances. God may well have allowed the trials and attacks for the very purpose of turning us back to Him from our path of self determination and self-sufficiency. He is continually seeking to draw us back to His presence, purpose, protection and provision, but we must make every effort to cooperate. Like Paul, who wrote the command to rejoice in terrible circumstances while in prison not knowing whether he would live or die, we must learn to "rejoice in the Lord always," no matter how bad our situation may be. It turns our eyes from our problems and our self and draws us closer to Him, where we find joy, peace and strength for the journey.

I'm sure Paul learned this principle while in chains in that Philippian jail when he and Silas chose to sing praises to the Lord rather than feel sorry for themselves or be paralyzed with fear (which would have been the natural response). Their decision to rejoice brought God's deliverance not only for themselves but for many others. No wonder the book of Philippians is called the epistle of joy because Paul used the words "joy" and "rejoice" often in order to emphasize their importance in our walk with God.

My wife, Susan, and I also experienced the truth of this principle many years ago in our early years of marriage and ministry. We felt like we were under attack from every direction, having problems in our family, finances, health and things weren't going well in the church. This soon led us to the conclusion (with plenty of help from the father of lies, I'm sure!) that God was mad at us because we had done something wrong. Though we could not think of anything and knew we had been working hard to serve the Lord faithfully in rather stressful circumstances, we tried to repent of whatever came to mind but to no avail.

Suddenly, it occurred to us that God knows our hearts and His grace is greater than all our mistakes. Maybe we were under attack because we were doing something right, because we've been making great efforts and some progress in following Christ and advancing the Kingdom. Rather than being discouraged, defeated and feeling sorry for ourselves, perhaps we should celebrate that the devil is mad and maybe even a little afraid of how God might use us.

We began to rejoice, as the early disciples, "that we had been counted worthy to suffer for His sake" and thank God for the privilege of being His children and servants. Actually, we decided to go out and have pizza (that's all we could afford at the time) as an act of celebration. Immediately, we came out from under the cloud of heaviness and began once again to enjoy the Lord's presence. Soon even our situation began to change, not only back to the way it was before all of the attacks but we also began going forward into God's good plan for our lives, family and church. It was almost like the devil decided, "I'm not going to give them cause to celebrate!" and he began to back off for a time.

It's easy to rejoice when things are going well and God seems to be present, but how we respond when everything seems to be falling apart and all hell breaks loose against us, reveals more about our relationship with God and our future destiny. The choice to rejoice even in the most difficult things life and/or the enemy brings our way is an act of faith, a sacrifice of praise born out of a heart of love and a desire to please and glorify the Lord whether by life or death. This kind of attitude gets His attention and brings His presence. God loves to come alongside and honor those who honor Him, which brings us to the second and most important blessing that comes from this principles of rejoicing.

James 4

The Word teaches us that "God inhabits the praises of His people." Since praise and worship from the heart is our way of drawing near to God, then we can be certain that He will also draw near to us. And when God shows up, the enemy must flee – "Let God arise and His enemies be scattered!" In making the choice to rejoice when everything around us is falling apart and everything in us feels like crying and giving up, we are inviting God into our circumstances. When He comes, we can be certain that something is going to change – either us, our situation or both – and because He loves us we can trust that it will change for the good.

28

Trust in the Lord With all your Heart

Maybe that's what it all comes down to, the determining factor on whether or not we will walk with God and stay close to Him through the problems for life – do we really trust Him? In choosing to rejoice even in the most trying times, we are choosing to trust in God and believe His promises. It is an act of faith, a decision to not be turned from my path toward and with the Lord no matter how I feel or how bad it appears. But how often do we choose to go with our erratic feelings or our confused thoughts, which so frequently lead us on a path away from God?

That we would choose to trust our emotions and/or our natural reasoning above the King of kings and Lord of lords, the Creator of all things is either the ultimate act of pride or total insanity (or both!). How could we put our trust in our erratic feelings or confused minds that often change as quickly as our Michigan weather? And yet, if you're anything like me, no matter how fickle these so called "friends" might be, we are more committed to them than the One who has loved us with an everlasting love and is always there for us with our best interest in mind.

It's hard to break old habits and say good-bye to old friends no matter how many times they've hurt us and led us astray. They may not be satisfying but at least they're familiar and we're comfortable. So, like the Israelites, whenever life gets difficult (which happens often in a fallen world controlled by the enemy), we want to go back to Egypt. Rather than trusting and following the One who has set us free and is bringing us into an amazing place where we will be with Him forever, we often choose to let fear and frustration (this isn't as easy as I thought it would be!) turn us back to the old way. Lord, please leave me alone and let me go back to trying to muddle through constructing the life I think is best for me...

No wonder God commands us in His Word to "trust in the Lord with all your heart and do not lean on your own understanding." He goes on to say that if we will acknowledge His presence and sovereignty as we navigate through our days, He will direct our path – He will make known to us the path of abundant and eternal life! Furthermore, He tells us that this path leads directly into His presence where we will find the fullness of joy and pleasure forever! It certainly sounds better than the fleeting moments of fun and the occasional glimpses of happiness mixed in with a whole lot of work and trouble I've found on my way. Still it's mine and I find it hard to give it up. After all, my breakthrough might be just around the next corner. Though the trail is getting darker and more painful, we take every little ray of light as a sign that God may soon bless our chosen road to success.

Prov. 3:5,6
Ps. 16:11

Could it be that those few moments when the light breaks through are one of God's way of saying that He's still with us and that He's showing us the way back to Him before we crash and burn? I was one of those stubborn ones who, of course, insisted on taking the hard way because I was so confident in my own ability to figure it out, to handle whatever comes along. Oh, how wrong I was! It was like God took His hand off and said, "Ok, if you want to persist on this path and ignore all my warnings, then go ahead and see where it leads. I'll be there to pick up the pieces when you hit the wall." Like Peter, there had to be a thorough breaking (or perhaps I should say crushing) of my self-confidence before I would surrender to God's will and way. Only then did I put my hope and trust fully in Him.

I wish I could say that is where it has stayed all these years in my walk with Him, but like so many people, I often fall back into the old habits of trusting in my own ability to make a plan and work my plans (or as John Eldredge says in Walking with God wanting my "nice little life" and then trying to "make it happen"). If trusting the Lord with all my heart is the key to walking with Him on the path of life, then we can be certain it will be our place of battle. Between the flesh and the devil, the simple act of trusting God can be quite difficult, requiring much work and warfare.

But if trust is what it all comes down to, then it's worth the effort and the fight no matter what it takes.

I am convinced that for me and for most people it's time to settle it in your heart. If Jesus is truly the best way, the right way and the only way to God and the awesome life He has for us, then it's worth giving our all. Let's stop playing the free agent market hoping to find a better deal. As long as you're keeping your options open, the enemy will be right there with his latest deal trying to convince you that he has something better and easier than following Jesus. And it may seem that way for a time.

If you don't settle it in your heart and mind, you'll be the double-minded person that James declares to be unstable in all his/her ways. He further adds that such a person is like a wave that one minute reaches out in faith but soon falls back in unbelief, and is tossed by the winds of circumstances and understanding. Perhaps this is the very reason many will fall away in the perilous times of the last days. As long as you remain uncommitted to the Lord and His will for your life, you will be vulnerable to the deception of the evil one and in constant danger of wandering off or turning away from God when the journey gets hard. Like the Israelites during the Exodus, you'll either be seeking something better or wanting to go back to your bondage as soon as you hit the next trial.

James 1:7

Why do you think Jesus asked, "When the Son of Man returns, will He find faith on the earth?" Maybe it was because He saw the tendency of His own disciples to frequently give in to doubt and unbelief even after they had seen Him do so many miracles. I'm sure He was also aware of the trouble that would come upon the earth before His return. No wonder God brought in the Faith Movement to strengthen us for the days ahead and prepare us for His coming. Unfortunately, many took this message as a means to get what they wanted from God, and so it became an acquiring faith rather than an enduring faith. What happens when things aren't going the way we want and believed they would?

I saw this often in our prison ministry where many excitedly embraced the faith message as a way to get whatever they asked as long as they determined not to doubt. Naturally, the first thing they began to believe for was to get out of prison and then they did their very best to follow the formula of positive confession while remaining convinced of a positive outcome. Imagine the disappointment when they were turned down at the parole board. Now they became equally convinced that this "stuff" doesn't work, especially if

Mk. 11:23-24

they were turned down a second time; thus many walked away from the faith.

It reminds me of when John the Baptist was in prison awaiting his execution and he sent his disciples to Jesus to ask if He was really the expected One, the Messiah, the Savior, or should they look for another. This was after John had already declared Jesus to be "the Lamb of God who takes away the sin of the world!" But now things were going from bad to worse and perhaps he needed some confirmation to alleviate his doubts, which is understandable considering the gravity of his situation. Jesus, however, did not directly answer his question but instead challenged him with a statement that echoes to us today. He said, "Go and report to John what you have seen and heard…" (I.e. all the miracles and the gospel being preached). Then Jesus added something that seems almost out of context, but is actually very appropriate and powerful for John and all who come into difficult circumstances – "Blessed is he who does not take offense at me."

What do you do when life comes at you like a freight train and it not only knocks you down but every car seems to take another piece of you as it goes by? Have you ever had one of those times when everything seems to be going wrong, and everyone seems to be against you? It's a very lonely place that we all have visited from time to time, and how we handle these severe trials may determine whether or not we make it to the end and are prepared for the Lord's return or whether we become one of the many who fall away in the last days.

As we read about the perilous times, the birth pangs and the tribulations of the last days, it is evident that only those who are established in the faith will be able to endure and overcome. If we can't handle the stress of daily life and the general warfare that goes with it, how will we stand in the pressure and intensity of the final days and end times battles? Even now we are being tested and prepared for those times, and God is looking for those through whom He can display His awesome power and glory on the earth, as well as to the principalities and powers in the heavenly places. These are the ones whom Daniel declares will "know their God and do great exploits."

So, my dear brothers and sisters, I challenge you now as we see the day coming, to settle it in your heart that you will trust and serve the Lord no matter what happens in your life in the days ahead. Like Jesus, we must "set our face like flint," as we press on to know and follow the Lord. This is the attitude of someone who is established in the faith, convinced that the Lord is everything He says He is much more and that only He has the words and path of life.

Job had this kind of faith when in the midst of his severe trials he boldly declared, "though He slay me, yet will I trust him". He could say that in the midst of his great suffering (and yes, his times of questioning and complaining!) because he truly believed that God's Redeemer would triumph over Satan, sin and suffering. Furthermore, he would share in that victory through a physical resurrection by which he would see and dwell with God forever. This hope enabled Job to see that his trials, as painful as they may be, would serve as preparation and purification for that glorious day because he held fast to the truth of His word.

Trusting God and His Word in the midst of difficult times will not only enable us to make it all the way to the end, but it will also bring us there "perfect and complete, lacking nothing." As people who have been refined and matured by what the Lord sends or allows to come our way, we will be prepared to joyfully do His will until the day He comes to receive us to Himself fully and forever. Those who just "sort of" trust God as long as things are going the way they want or think they should, will never fully achieve their destiny. They will probably not even make it to the end, especially if you consider all that is coming upon the earth before the Lord finally returns to fully establish His rule and reign.

We need to develop the kind of faith that Daniel and his three friends (Shadrach, Meshach and Abednego) had in the midst of a pagan society. Daniel remained faithful to his times of prayer even though it caused him to be thrown into the lion's den because he trusted that his God was well able to deliver him since he had not done anything wrong. His three amigos went even further with their faith by declaring that while God was able to protect them, they would still choose to serve and worship Him even if He didn't deliver them. All of them were given a greater knowledge of the Lord's awesome power and thus became strong witnesses for God among the heathen as they rose to positions of great influence. In addition, Daniel was given incredible revelations of what would happen in the last days, which provide a road map for us today, thousand of years later.

In the times that are soon coming upon us, Satan will seek to wear out the saints and will be raging against God's people because he knows his time is short. Only those who know and trust their God will be strong and carry out great exploits as they prepare the way for the Lord's coming. These are people who have spent much time with Him and in His Word, so that they would consider it an honor to suffer or even die for His Kingdom and glory. Many around the world are already living in this level of trust as they seek to share the gospel in Muslim, Hindu, Buddhist and other unevangelized and persecuted nations. God is very pleased with such a display of love and trust whether by living or dying for Him. Where do we find and develop the kind of trust that will not only enable us to make it to the end, but do all He calls us to do in the exciting last days before His return?

29

Communication is the key: Know and Do the Word

Whenever I do pre-marital counseling with a couple, I always ask them what they think is the key to having a great relationship. Almost without exception their answer is communication. Then I ask them if I lined up 100 Christian couples, what would they say about their communication. To this I get various answers, but the answer I give them really gets their attention. Most of the men would probably say, "I don't know, but it seems OK to me." About 80% of the women, on the other hand, would probably say, "We have little or no meaningful communication," if they are willing to be honest. No wonder our marriages are failing at the same rate as those in the world. Men are distant and in many cases oblivious to the needs of their wives and women are frustrated (and yes, desperate!) to the point that they will nag, whine, criticize and complain until they finally give up and watch "soaps" to get a vicarious thrill, before they decide to make a change. During this time men lose themselves in their work, hobbies or addictions rather than face their fears and need to change. Finally they often give in to temptation and find someone who "understands" them. But that is another story, another book...

The point I'm trying to make is that our relationship with the Lord (and everyone else, for that matter) is only as good as our communication with Him. Many claim to know and love Jesus while making little or no effort to pray or read His Word, thinking that an hour or two in church each week is enough (though they often sleep or daydream through it!). Does that level of intercourse show a desire to know Him in an intimate way or is it simply a reflection of the pervading attitude in our society, which is do the bare minimum to get what we want from Him.

Reflecting back on the days when I was first saved, as I seek to return to my first love, I remember the hunger I had for the Word of God. I was in church or Bible study every chance I could get, and I had to read something from God's word every day. It was so easy and so exciting because I wanted to learn all I could about the Lord and His ways. In that first year I read through the entire Bible, and in addition, I read through the New Testament two and a half times because I especially wanted to know more about Jesus. The words just seemed to jump off the page and went right into my heart as I prayed and asked the Lord to reveal Himself to me. It was easy to be obedient to the things I was reading because I meekly received them as the Word of the Lord and it continued to change me day by day.

Mt. 4:4

Thankfully, I developed a positive habit, a godly discipline of reading God's Word every day and reading through the entire Bible every year that I have been a Christian. Of course there are some days that I am not able to read, but I always get back to it as soon as possible, knowing that His Word is truth and life to the believer, our daily bread. Jesus reminds us of this when He answers Satan's attack by quoting a verse from Deuteronomy 8:3, "Man does not live by bread alone, but by every word that proceeds from the mouth of God." By this statement He was declaring God's Word to be our protection and provision that is more necessary even than the food we eat.

This was very evident to me when I first came to the Lord in the midst of a painful divorce. While I often had trouble eating or sleeping, I had no problem reading the Bible. As God's love and truth jumped off the pages to penetrate my heart and mind, I continued to devour the Word, feeling like I couldn't get enough. It amazed me how the Lord continually spoke directly to me and my specific circumstances, which I found out later is called a "rhema" word (the same as Matthew 4:4) as opposed to "logos" which is the general knowledge of God and the Bible as a whole. As I prayerfully read God's Word with an open heart and mind, He began to teach me the things I needed to know when I needed to know them and so much more.

Paul declared to the Romans, "Oh, the depth of the riches both of the wisdom and knowledge of God!" I prayed for God to continue to reveal Himself as well as His will and ways to me, and that He would give me the wisdom to know how to love and obey Him. As it says in Ephesians 1:17-19, I prayed that the lord would give me "a spirit of wisdom and revelation in the knowledge of Him, and that the eyes of my heart would be enlightened to know the hope of His calling, the riches of the glory of His inheritance, and the exceeding greatness of His power toward us who believe..."

This was such a blessed time for me as the Lord showed the truth of His Word, the love of Jesus, and the power of the Holy Spirit to bring healing to my broken heart and draw me closer to Him. Truly I felt like I was becoming His friend as He opened my understanding and made known to me some of the mysteries of the kingdom in Christ "in whom are hidden all the treasures of wisdom and knowledge." The more I would draw close to Him and seek to know Him through prayer and His Word, the more He would draw close and reveal Himself to me. In spite of the mistakes that come from youthful inexperience and immaturity, I felt Him close to me, patiently teaching me His ways through all the joys and trials of following Him.

Col. 2:3

Oh, that I would have maintained this level of communication and closeness! In the busyness and stress of life and ministry it's so easy to take the relationship for granted, to put it on cruise control and go on memories without even realizing you're losing the passion and intimacy you once had. Thankfully, the depth and commitment that developed has kept me through this time, along with the godly habits I established in the beginning of my walk with the Lord. But I know it's time to rekindle the fire.

Just like my relationship with my wife after many years of marriage, it's easy to settle into patterns and routines, and to think I know her so well that I know what she's going to say even before she opens her mouth. Of course, that is not true and she continues to surprise and amaze me as I really listen and give her an opportunity to share what's on her heart and mind. So, I am asking the Lord to stir me and shake me out of my comfortable place with her and Him. (Do you realize what a dangerous prayer that is? I can't begin to tell you how radically my life has changed just in the past year or so, and how rapidly everything continues to change for me and in the world!). When I read the Word, I pray that He will open it up in greater depth of understanding and breadth of application.

That has been the best part about listening to the Lord through His Word. Not only has it revealed more of Him and His ways, but I have also learned so much about me and my ways. I have found scripture to be both a mirror that gives me a clear picture of what I look like to Him and a scope that is able to focus on important details that need immediate attention.

I am not implying that we are always under God's microscope so He can find every little thing that's wrong in order to punish and condemn us for it – nothing could be further from the truth! Much of what He shows me about myself are the good things He has placed in me and the awesome plan He has for me, which enable me to combat the constant condemnation of the enemy and myself. It also gives me the courage and incentive to recognize those things that need to change (yes, there's still plenty of them!) and be willing to cooperate in the process.

Knowing that the Lord's purpose always includes restoration and relationship, I am able to face the reality of my significant need to change without becoming discouraged or depressed. As the Word reveals my need to change, the Spirit leads me to repent and enables me to forsake that path in order to more fully follow the Lord. Then, by hiding God's Word in my heart, it is easier to recognized and resist both the lies of the enemy and the rationalizations of the flesh in order to stay on the path. When Satan tempted Jesus, even using scripture and half truths, Jesus quickly countered with the truth, "It is written..." Only as we study, memorize and meditate on God's Word will we be able to stand against the lies of the enemy that are being unleashed in these last days which as causing many to fall away – that is, if we also learn how to put his word in to practice.

Jesus said that those who continue in the truth, which means to abide, live, or dwell in His Word by submitting to Him and committing to His teaching, will be true disciples. They are the ones who will learn and know Him and His ways by experience, as they walk it out, and it will be the truth that makes (sets and keeps) them free of the lies and bondage of the devil. It's not enough to get His Word into our head, but we must get it into our heart by applying it to our life. Then we will be able to walk in freedom and victory.

This will be especially important in the days that are fast coming upon us, the perilous times preceding the Lord's return. At the end of His most famous discourse, the Sermon on the Mount, Jesus concluded His teaching with a very strong warning to those He knew would soon face much trouble, persecution and suffering. In light of the storms that inevitably come in all of our lives and are coming upon the whole world, it is crucial that we both hear and do anything and everything He has told and will tell us. He likens those people to the wise man who built his house on the rock so that it was firmly established and did not fall. How essential this is for us upon whom is coming the very end of the age and the final great battles and judgments!

The alternative seems so foolish – to build our house, our life on the shifting sands of popular opinion and worldly wisdom. And yet, so many in our nation will take the message of Oprah, Dr. Phil, CNN or their favorite actor or rock star over the truth of God's Word. They have heard enough to consider it to be occasionally helpful, but they have also determined that obedience is optional according to what they believe is relevant and necessary . A large majority in America do not acknowledge that the Bible is God's absolute truth and final authority. Instead they have chosen to adopt or construct their own relative truth which allows them to live however they want. Thus, we see the decay and destruction of the Christian foundation of our nation, which will not (is not) hold us when the storms come. As Jesus concludes, "great was the fall" of those who would not hear or do his word.

It is essential then to prayerfully read, study, memorize, meditate on and then do all of God's Word if we are going to stand and be ready for all that's coming. We need a whole lot more of scripture in us than an occasional sermon, a yearly conference and some casual Bible reading will provide. I challenge you to listen to and read the Word of God as if your life depended on it! His Word is life and the truth that will make us free and has the power to change us and defeat our enemy.

30

My Sheep Hear My Voice and Follow Me

While the Word of God is the final authority and the standard by which we judge all truth, God has always spoken and still speaks to His people. If we are going to walk with God on the path of life, away from all deception, darkness and destruction, we will need to cultivate the ability to hear His voice. To all of the seven churches in Revelation, Jesus closes His letter with the challenge, "He who has an ear to hear, let Him hear what the Spirit says to the churches." That implies the Spirit is still speaking and we need to open our spiritual ears, which means to listen intently with the determination to obey whatever he says.

Truly we are living in a very serious and crucial hour as we approach the coming of the Lord and all that we must do to prepare the way for Him in our hearts and in the world around us. There is no doubt that we need to be carefully watching and listening so that we will know what God is doing and saying to His people.

The Lord says in His Word that "He will do nothing without first revealing His secret to His servants the prophets". The difficulty is that there are so many in our nation claiming to be prophets, and they are presenting such a wide range of messages regarding God's present and future dealings. If we are only relying on others to tell us what God is saying, especially if we are using the internet or conferences or

Amos 3:7
Mt. 24:11
Jn. 10:3-5
II Thes.5:17

other avenues in which it is impossible to know the character and track record of the messenger, there will be much confusion and deception. In fact, Jesus said that the time before His return would be distinguished by the number of false messengers and those who would be led astray – "many false prophets will rise up and deceive many."

So, each of us must learn to hear the voice of the Lord clearly and then seek confirmation from the few, mature, trusted advisors that God places in our lives. Be sure they are people who are willing to speak the truth and won't just tell you what you want to hear. This is no time to look for those who will scratch our itching ears, but seek people who love you enough to speak the Word of the Lord even when it hurts and makes you angry. It's better to painfully examine your life and circumstances than to happily proceed in a lie.

Jesus is calling us all back to His initial commands – "Repent, Believe and Come, Follow me!" In order to be true followers of Jesus Christ we must learn to distinguish His voice among the many voices calling and even shouting for our attention. As the world, flesh and the devil get louder in the last days in an effort to draw us away from God's path, it is essential for us to be able to carefully listen for and truly hear the still small voice of the Lord. This truth was made evident when Jesus told His followers that His sheep would hear His voice and follow Him as He calls them by name and leads them, but they would not follow a stranger for they did not know his voice.

The key, then, is to learn how to hear His voice anywhere and anytime. For most of us that will require some fine tuning in order to remove all the static around us, which is easier (though far from automatic) in church or in the times we are doing our devotions. However, as we go throughout our day in the busyness of our work and lives, this can be a real problem. So often we rush through our week, taking our lives into our own hands by making a plan and working our plan, without ever stopping to inquire of the Lord. Even worse, we get so busy and so intent on accomplishing our purpose that we fail to hear or refuse to recognize God's attempt to adjust our course. Perhaps this is the reason Paul said to "pray without ceasing."

It reminds me of the story of Balaam who started out right by seeking the Lord's direction and obeying His voice, but soon headed for trouble. Convinced the Lord was giving him the desires of his heart (wealth and prestige), he excitedly followed the servants to King Balak. Knowing that his motives were not right and that he was on a fast track to destruction, the Lord attempted to block his path and get his attention along the way with the help of his faithful donkey who had ears to hear and eyes to see. God finally spoke to Balaam through the donkey, which should have been all that was needed to finally get him to stop and listen, but it only made him angry enough to beat the animal and threaten to kill him. The Lord finally opened Balaam's eyes to see the angel with his sword drawn, which at least temporarily got his attention. The rest of the story tells us that Balaam eventually found a way to achieve his goal, which caused the death of some of God's people and led him to his own destruction.

Many Christians today have said that they rarely or never hear the voice of the Lord. Could this be like the days of Samuel when the word of the Lord was rare; there was no widespread revelation because of the sin that was so prevalent even in the priesthood? Or are we in the time that Amos spoke of when the Lord would send a famine of hearing His words? Certainly we see many running to and fro to ministers, meetings or the media and they either come away with what they want to hear or a lot of confusion from the variety of messages. But who knows for sure what God is saying to His people in this crucial time?

I Sam. 3:1
Amos 8:11, 12
Lk. 11:1

I can not emphasize enough how absolutely critical it is for each one of us to learn how to wait on the Lord, listen intently to all that He says, and then quickly and completely obey Him. All through the Bible and throughout history every man or woman who walked closely with God and was mightily used for His Kingdom was a person of prayer. Jesus was the ultimate example of how to pray often, intensely and sometimes even all through the night.

Knowing that Jesus' incredible power, wisdom and guidance came from his connection to the Father, His disciples asked Him, "Lord, teach us to pray." It would most definitely be wise for us to do the same, and then take time to listen and fully learn what He tells us. Instead of just repeating the outline and model prayer Jesus gave us, wouldn't it be much better to simply communicate with Him along these lines and allow the Spirit to fill in the details? The key, though, is to spend time with Him and allow Him to instruct us in this essential Christian art and discipline without trying to come up with some new method or program to make it happen.

If we are going to get back to Jesus and our first love for Him, it must start with focusing our eyes and ears on Him and turning away from all distractions. Elijah was reminded that God was heard as a still, small voice and not in all the noise and commotion around us. How crucial will it be for us to be dialed in to the sound of God's voice in order to safely navigate through the events of these last days staying close to Him! It will certainly force those who have been following at a distance to press into His presence or run the risk of falling away and being left behind. And those who have been accustomed to getting their itching ears scratched by only what they want to hear will have to learn to refocus on what the Lord is saying even when it may seem difficult or frightening. This will require us to trust that whatever is coming and whatever the Lord calls us to do, He will be with us and enable us to finish our course and the good work He has for us.

31

Encourage One Another All the More...

We are going to need one another even more as we begin to approach the last days and the coming of the Lord. In fact the perilous times we are entering into will force us to finally answer Jesus' prayer in John 17. Four times in three verses He prays for His followers "that they may be one" just as He and the Father are in perfect unity. This will enable the world to believe that Jesus is the One sent from God and that He loves them just as the Bible has said.

Knowing that unity is crucial for the pouring out of God's Spirit and the full revelation of Jesus Christ to a lost and dying world, the enemy has done all that he can to prevent it from happening. As we look at all the fighting and quarreling along with the many divisions down through the years, we would have to conclude that Satan has been pretty effective. In fact, all the denominations we have in our country today, most of which refuse to do anything with the others, certainly indicates that the church has lost this battle. Most do not even consider unity a priority and are doing nothing to work toward answering Jesus' prayer, which so strongly reveals what's on His heart.

I can't help but believe that this is one of the main reasons the church has lost its power and witness in the world today. As we fight and pull away from one another, we are also pulling away from God who has made us one family. And how can the world believe that God loves them if His children can't even get along? The hypocrisy and hostility that is so prevalent in our churches is giving people plenty of excuses not to come and is causing them to leave by the thousands. Unless God intervenes, the church in America will be mostly empty and the remaining attendees will have very little love or life.

It's definitely time for the church to begin to reverse this trend or we will become irrelevant in our society and face extinction. We may not yet be on the endangered species list, but we are fast approaching the place where we might need to call for the paddles to shock us back to life. Perhaps that is exactly what the Lord is doing by allowing the pre-tribulation birth pangs that we have already seen coming up on the earth. I have a strong feeling that soon we will put away all labels, the pride, and all the doctrines that divide us and then we need to determine to live and work together with all who love Jesus for His glory. Our very survival, not to mention the fulfillment of our purpose, may well depend on our willingness to lay aside our differences and diligently pull together for the sake of our Lord and His Kingdom.

The writer of the book of Hebrews (10:19-25) gives three strong admonitions to the church that are especially appropriate for us in these last days – "let us draw near… let us hold fast the confession of our hope… let us consider one another…" I have already written about our need to draw close to the Lord and to learn to trust Him with all of our heart in order to be ready for His coming. But have we truly made an effort to consider, to carefully think about and understand, how much we need one another in the Body of Christ?

God must have known about our tendency toward pride and independence when He included all the "one another" passages in the Bible. I challenge you to take a concordance and find all the "one another" scriptures in the New Testament and prayerfully see what the Lord is saying to you through them. If you don't come away with a profound realization that God designed us to need each other, as well as Him, and that it's His desire for His family to get along, then I would have to wonder about the condition of your heart (and head!).

In this particular passage in Hebrews the writer warns us not to "forsake the assembling of ourselves together, as is the manner of some." Every pastor will readily admit the reality of this statement in the church today. Whether it's the busyness of our schedules, the boredom of the religious routine, or the lack of love and commitment to God and His people (or all of the above!), many people come and go as they please. There is usually a faithful few who can be counted on not only to be there but to be actively involved in the work of the ministry. However, the majority are sporadic in their attendance and rarely offer nor can they be relied upon to help. Most come if and when they need something from God or others without even considering that they might be needed to serve others.

No wonder the passage also said to "stir up love and good works." As we come together with others who love the Lord, it greatly strengthens our passion to love and serve Him and others. It's hard to remain committed when you spend most of your time around unbelievers or nominal Christians. We are exhorted to "encourage one another all the more as we see the Day approaching."

Brothers and Sisters, the Day of His coming is rapidly drawing near and so we need to draw near to Him and to each other. This is not the time to be fussing and fighting or focusing on the minor doctrinal differences that only serve to weaken and divide us. Believe me, in the days that are coming, we won't be pridefully looking at labels or perfection, but we will only be concerned about the heart and whether or not we can discern the Spirit within others. As we seek to establish and maintain the unity of the Spirit in the bond of peace, "God Himself will bring us into the unity of the faith... to a perfect man to the measure of the stature of the fullness of Christ."

The early church had this level of fellowship. In fact they had "all things in common" in that they didn't hang on to their possessions but would sell them and provide for those who were in need. This prepared them for the persecution that would soon come strongly against the church, since they were already learning how to work together and take care of each other. Such unity also was an incredible witness to the world and thus brought in a great harvest of souls. As long as we continue to persist in the spirit of independence and division, we will not be prepared to handle the perilous times coming upon the world let alone gather in the last days harvest that is promised.

Certainly the tribulation and judgments prophesied in scripture which are already evident in the world today, will force us to pull together as a family. Knowing how much we will need one another in the days ahead, it will begin to squeeze us into the answer to Jesus' prayer in John 17. But I'm concerned that those who are not already in that mindset and moving in a direction toward unity may also be squeezed out by the pressure of the end times. If they have not yet recognized the importance of the Body of Christ, and they have resisted God's efforts to bring them into covenant relationship, they will be susceptible to the ant-Christ system in their time of great need.

Heb. 10:22-25
Eph. 4:3
Eph. 4:13
Ecc. 4:9-12

In Ecclesiastes 4:9-12, Solomon makes it clear that together we are better. Those who are walking and working with others rather than trying and thinking they can make it on their own will be more productive, protected, passionate and powerful, especially when they are joined together in Christ. He enables us to love, forgive and have patience with one another so that our unity in Him is not easily broken, as we see so often in both the world and the church today. We can pick each other up when we fall or stumble but "woe to him who is alone when he falls." Also, it is so much easier to stay committed and passionate for the Lord and the work He has called us to when there are others to encourage us along the way.

I want to make it very clear that in the times that are quickly coming upon us, if we are going to be ready for the return of the Lord and all He wants us to do beforehand, fellowship is not optional. It is absolutely essential for us to be closely connected with others in the Body of Christ. The Greek word "koinonia," which is translated as "fellowship" in the Bible, literally means to have all things in common, which is much more than attending a church or going to a meeting.

Perhaps the closest things in our world today to true fellowship would be a circle of good friends who know each other very well and spend time together individually and as families. These are people you can count on to help you in your times of need, to fight with you and for you in your battles, and to stick with you through your trials and even your mistakes. If you are fortunate enough to have this kind of fellowship already, know that it is a rare and precious commodity and be diligent to maintain and help it grow.

The truth is that very few churches provide for this kind of close connection. We keep people busy with meetings and programmed activities but there is very little depth in our relationships. When you add in all the busyness of our work and outside activities, especially if you have children, there is not enough time or energy left to build good friendships. There may be a group we see more often at meetings, but how well do we really know them or do they know us? Especially in the larger churches, we may make a few casual acquaintances but mostly we remain strangers who may recognize the face but may not even know their name, let alone the details of their life and family.

This is the reason that many churches have gone to home groups in order to develop closer fellowship within the Body of Christ. To get away from people just going to church and trying to establish the mindset of being the church, they have had to think outside the box, outside the building and the traditional organizational structure. In many ways it has brought us back to the early church which met in the temple and from house to house. Because of this the Body of Christ was able to grow rapidly both in numbers and maturity. By being in close fellowship they were also able to be strong in discipleship – literally pouring out their lives and the Spirit that was in them into the lives of the new converts.

Not only for the fulfillment of the great commission, to go and make disciples (more than just getting people to make a decision), but for our own survival in these last days, the church must get back to true Biblical unity. As with the persecuted church in many nations in the world today, we will need to have a network of people who are ready to care for one another and even fight and die for each other if necessary. All the man-made labels and divisions will quickly disintegrate and we will be able to see each other as family and as brothers and sisters in Christ. Don't you think it's time for that to happen after all these years of quarreling, fighting and dividing?

32

The Great Commission

Eph. 2:10
Luke 1
Luke 19:10
Acts 1:8
Mt. 24:46
II Pet. 3:9
Mt. 24:14
Lk. 14:21, 23

As we determine to spend time with the Lord and draw close to Him, He will speak to us and lead us into the good works that He has planned and prepared for us to walk in. In other words, we are not down here hanging on by our fingernails saying, "Even so, come Lord Jesus!" Jesus said to occupy or do business until He comes. That means He has much for us to do before He returns, and rather than simply waiting for His coming, we need to be as He was – "busy about the Father's business."

While He was on the earth, Jesus invited His disciples to join Him in the family business: "Follow me and I will make you fishers of men." All that He taught them, by word and by example, was designed to do more than just prepare them for heaven. He continually trained them how to reach others so that they would carry on His mission, which He declared was "to seek and save the lost."

Just in case they might have forgotten or did not fully understand, Jesus gave them (and us) what has become known as the Great Commission. The last verses of both Matthew and Mark include His command to "Go and make disciples." They were to do this by preaching the gospel, baptizing those who believe, teaching them to obey all that He has commanded, and releasing healing and deliverance to all who need to be set free. Luke adds that they were to first wait for the Promise of the Father, which he declares to be the pouring out of the Spirit in Acts. This coming of the Holy Spirit would enable and empower them to be His witnesses wherever He would send them, even to the ends of the earth.

All that we are doing in these last days to prepare for the Lord's coming should somehow be connected to the great commission. Our focused purpose and determined effort should be to reach people, bring them to the saving knowledge of Jesus Christ, and then do all we can to help prepare them for heaven. In His powerful message on the end times in Matthew 24, Jesus closes with a challenge to be a faithful and wise servant He both defines and inspires us with the statement, "blessed is the servant whom his master finds doing His will when He comes."

While God's will is unique in many ways for each one of us, in that He has a special plan for every person, there is also a common calling. We know for certain that it is His will that "none should perish but that all should come to repentance." God so longs for His children to return to Him that He has delayed the return of Jesus until "this gospel of the kingdom is preached in the entire world as a witness to all the nations." Jesus is waiting until His house is filled and the celebration can begin. Since many continue to make excuses why they can't come, He commands His servants to find the least and the lowest, to "go out into the highways and hedges and compel them to come in." Knowing the desire of the Master and the lateness of the hour, we should be doing all we can to share Jesus. Our purpose should be not just to make it to heaven but to bring as many with us as we can.

I once heard a statistic that totally blew me away. It stated that 80% of all people in America who call themselves a Christian had never led even one person to the Lord. That said more to me about the state of American Christianity than anything else I had seen or heard. How could anyone have read the Bible or attended church and not know that we are commanded to "Go and make disciples"? Even more, how could anyone receive the amazing love of our Lord Jesus Christ and not want to share it with everyone they know or meet? Either there's a terrible lack of understanding of Biblical Christianity in our nation or many who claim to be Christians don't really know the One they claim to follow (or both).

For us to be ready for the Lord's return, this is one area that will have to radically change, individually and corporately. In many churches their only attempt at evangelism is to put a sign outside the church with their meeting times and perhaps some catchy little phrase. We're not here on the earth to have nice little Sunday services and then leave with nobody changed and nothing to do until next week. We have been given a mission, a good work to do, and we will be held accountable for what we've done with what we've been given. God will come looking for fruit. Those who bear fruit will hear, "Well done!" and be rewarded for their labor. Those who don't might be saved as if by fire or they might hear, "Depart from me you wicked and lazy servant. I never knew you."

It must also be understood that the Lord is expecting us to do more than just reach people for Christ. While bringing others to the place where they can make a decision to follow Jesus is the essential starting point, it is certainly not the end. Jesus said to make disciples, which means a disciplined follower both of the teacher and His teachings. That is why the great commission goes beyond preaching the gospel to baptizing them and teaching them to obey all that He has commanded. He wants His followers to be totally committed (immersed) to Him and to learn how to know His will and how to walk in His ways.

Whatever else God may have for us, we know that it is His will that we would be both saved and sanctified. This means that we must make that first step of faith to confess our sin and receive Jesus as our Savior and then determine to follow Him as Lord. As we spend time with Jesus and walk with Him, we will more and more be set apart from the flesh and the world unto God and, thus, we will become more like Him. It is our greatest privilege and responsibility to "grow up into our salvation", to "work out our salvation with fear and trembling" "so that we are "transformed from glory to glory into the image of Jesus Christ."

I Thes. 4:3
I Pet. 2:12
Phil. 2:12
II Cor. 3:18

The more we grow and mature in our faith, the more we will want and be able to help others grow as well. As absurd as it would be to have a baby and leave them to grow on their own, why would we get someone to make a decision for Christ without helping them to continue on in their faith? Yet this is exactly what happens in many churches and with many individuals. We proudly proclaim the number of people we got to "pray the sinner's prayer" but we rarely have a plan or are wiling to make the effort necessary to help them walk out their decision to follow Christ. Consequently, we have churches full of spiritual babies and many who have fallen away from the faith because of the opposition of the enemy and having no one to stand with them or fight for them. And once they have tasted of the Lord, tried to live the Christian life and then fall away, they are much harder to reach again for Jesus. They often say "I tried that and it didn't work for me."

So, then, the real work God has called us to is to make true disciples, disciplined followers of Jesus Christ, which is the greatest lack in the American church today. We have a fair amount of attendees and a few who are even committed enough to be members, but who is willing to go wherever Jesus leads and do whatever He asks? And who is willing to mentor and pour their lives into others so that they, too, learn how to walk with Jesus all the way to the end? Even as Jesus lived to please the Father and gave His life for others, we are called to do what pleases the Lord and to willingly (even sacrificially) shine His light, speak His truth and share His love with those He directs us to or puts in our path.

33

Abide in the Vine!

Everyone who calls himself a Christian must know that we will one day stand before the judgment seat of Christ to be held accountable for what we have done with what we've been given. Understanding this truth Paul "made it his aim to be well pleasing to the Lord." He further declares His purpose to first know Jesus in a deeper more intimate way and to make Him known to others. Realizing he would one day stand before His Lord he adds, "Knowing, therefore, the terror of the Lord, we persuade men." Those who would be ready for His return must cultivate this same zeal to draw close to Jesus, become like Him and help as many as they can to know Jesus as well.

The Bible makes it very clear that we are all called to bear fruit for the Lord. Our original commission in the garden was to "be fruitful and multiply; fill the earth and subdue it, have dominion…" Even though man had not yet sinned opening the door for Satan's evil assault, God knew the battle was coming and, therefore, warned that it would take much work and warfare in order to advance His kingdom. Most of our effort should be directed toward staying close to the One who is our Source of power, provision and protection. Without Jesus' presence and help we have no chance of fulfilling our commission and probably will not even survive in this hostile environment.

II Cor. 5:9-11
Gen. 1:28
Jn. 15
Mt. 25:1-13
Eph. 5:18

It is the enemy's determined purpose to distract, deceive and discourage as many of God's children as possible in order to cut them off or get them to turn away and fall back from following the Lord. His only way of getting back at Jesus, who defeated and humiliated him through the cross and resurrection, is to work on us and seek to take us on his path of destruction and eternal separation from God.

In the parable of the vine, Jesus made it clear that we are to focus on and make every effort to abide in Him. This means we must do far more than to occasionally visit Him when we feel like it or need a little help. Abiding implies that we must remain, dwell, to actually live with Him throughout our day and life. We must make every effort to get and stay connected to Jesus, realizing that without Him we can do nothing to bear fruit for the Kingdom and will be in danger of withering so that we are cast out, thrown into the fire and burned. However, as we determine to stay close to the Lord and faithful to His Word, we have the promise that our prayers will be answered and that we will bear much fruit. In this way we will glorify God and prove to be His disciples.

Another end times parable Jesus told concerning the need to watch and prepare for His coming, speaks of ten virgins, half of whom were wise and the other half who were foolish. Those who were declared wise had plenty of oil to keep their lamps burning even when the bridegroom was delayed, while the foolish virgin's oil began to run low and their lamps were going out. When the cry was heard of the return of the bridegroom, they first tried to get some from the wise, but the wise would not give them their oil, so they scrambled around trying to buy some. Unfortunately, the bridegroom came while they were still unprepared and the door was shut to the wedding celebration. Though they cried out for the Lord to open the door for them, it was too late and the Lord answered that He did not know them.

If we are going to be people who are ready for Jesus' return, it is essential that we get and stay filled with the Holy Spirit. The Scripture commands us not only to receive but to be filled with the Spirit. The Greek meaning of the verse makes it clear that we are to continually be filled. Since we are imperfect vessels (cracked pots!) that tend to leak and we are often pouring into others (or should be!), we must keep on being filled in order to stay prepared for the Lord's coming and do all that He has called us to do in the meantime.

Most Christians have little or no understanding of our relationship with the Holy Spirit even though He is here with us while God is in heaven seated on the throne and Jesus is now seated at His right hand. Have you ever wondered how Jesus could say that He would never leave or forsake us and that He would be with us always even to the end of the age while also saying to His disciples (often!) that He would be leaving soon and it was to their benefit that He go? Jesus meant that He would be with us in the form of the Holy Spirit whom He sent when He ascended to the Father.

Jesus explained that His leaving would be to our advantage because He would send another Helper who would lead us in all truth and empower us to be and do all that God commands. "Another" means one that is just like me and yet separate and distinct in His operation and ministry. Helper is the Greek word "paraklete" and means to come alongside and assist. Jesus made it clear that we are not orphans, left to fend for ourselves until He returns, but the Holy Spirit dwells with us and will be in us… forever!

When Jesus commanded those first disciples to wait in persevering, unified prayer with earnest expectation for the Promise of the Father, they had no trouble being obedient. Since Jesus would be leaving soon, it was clear that they desperately needed all the help they could get. Receiving the Holy Spirit and being baptized or filled with the Spirit was not an option but an absolute necessity for them to ever hope to finish their course and the purpose to which they had been called. This truth must have been greatly accentuated when they watched Jesus ascend into heaven. The realization must have been overwhelming that they were on their own in the midst of enemy territory. I'm quite sure these dire circumstances greatly increased their motivation to obey the Lord's command to receive and then allow the Holy Spirit to have His way in their lives.

Perhaps that is also what it will take in these end times for us to be desperately crying out for and open to the latter rain, the latter day's outpouring of the Spirit. As the perilous times come and the birth pangs increase, signaling the soon return of our Lord Jesus Christ, we will all be scrambling to get ready. Like the early church who faced the all out attack of Satan to cut off the advance of the Kingdom, so the end times church will need great grace and great power against an enemy who will be raging because his time is short. But this nation and the church in America has turned its back on God for so long and become so cold and rebellious, it seems that only judgments and tribulations will waken, soften and focus us back to the Lord. None of the beautiful buildings, entertaining services or ingenious programs will hold us or even matter! God will be looking for (and so will people in the world!) those whose hearts are longing for Him and pressing into His truth and power.

God has promised that there will come a time of great shaking in the last days in order to remove from us all that is not of Him and to remove us from all that He has not called us to. So, we must hold everything loosely. If we're hanging onto our own desires or the things of this world, then we are in danger of being shaken out with them. Only what is of the Lord and His unshakeable Kingdom are worth clinging to and will not only hold up in the shaking, but will carry us through these troubled times. Jesus said that He is the vine and we are to abide in Him, which means to press into and stay closely connected to Him in order to receive the life and power not only to survive, but to also bear fruit as we prepare for His return.

In order to help us draw close and stay close to Him, God is shaking the world and pruning our lives. His purpose and desire is that we would stay closely connected to Jesus, who is the true vine, so that the life blood and power of the Spirit can freely flow in and through us. As we remain in intimate fellowship with Jesus and full of the oil of the Holy Spirit, we will be prepared for the Lord's coming and accomplish all He asks of us during these last days.

34

Led by the Spirit of God

Staying close to the Lord and fulfilling His purposes for our lives in these last days will require us to learn how to be increasingly led by the Holy Spirit. In Romans 8:14 Paul boldly declares that only those who are progressively and continually being led by the Spirit of God are the true, mature sons of God (no longer children!). These are Christians who have worked out and grown up into their salvation, who have gone on to maturity through the Word and the power of the Spirit. Paul goes on to say that all creation is eagerly waiting and groaning for the revealing of the sons of God with the earnest expectation that the consummation of our redemption will also be released into physical creation just as the fall brought all creation into corruption or decay.

Could this be the time that all of history and all of creation has been looking and longing for? Does the actual timing of these events depend on the willingness of God's people to diligently prepare for His return? Peter seems to indicate that those who are looking and preparing for the Lord's return can somehow hasten the coming of the day of God. As we live in a manner that seeks to please and honor Jesus while making every effort to finish the work He has called us to, it is possible that we will be preparing the way and speeding up the day of His return. For that to happen, however, we will have to learn how to let the Helper help, since it is evident that we can't do it on our own.

I can't help thinking that this is one of the reasons for the shaking and tribulations of the last days – to bring us to the end of ourselves. In the perilous times that are coming upon us, it will soon be obvious to everyone that all of our beautiful buildings, excellent programs, creative technology, etc. will not be sufficient to hold us or help us through. God is bringing us back to the realization that it's "not by might nor by power, but by His Spirit." We will put no trust in the resources and talents of men for our survival or success, and it will be clear to everyone that all that is accomplished is of God – all glory will go to Him and not to our great ideas or efforts.

It must be remembered, however, that the Holy Spirit has been fully available to everyone since the Day of Pentecost, but few have learned how to walk with Him. The truth is that most Christians do not even celebrate Pentecost in a way that is similar to Christmas and Easter because they view the outpouring of the Spirit as frosting on the cake. In other words, it was a nice addition but unnecessary for the enjoyment of the substance. How many actually realize that the coming of the Holy Spirit in power was and is an absolutely essential part of God's plan for His people both individually and corporately?

I Pet. 3:12
Zech. 3:6
Acts 4:31-33
Rev. 3:17

To think that we could possibly fulfill God's purposes for His church in our own efforts, without the full presence and power of the Holy Spirit, shows a great deal of pride, ignorance and/or stupidity. The last day's church, those who determine to be ready for the Lord's return, will know without a doubt that it is only the wisdom and power of the Holy Spirit that will enable us to be successful in our desire to honor the Lord in perilous times. We must desperately cry out for the last day's revival that is prophesied in the scriptures even as the early church pressed into God's promise. Without the great grace and great power and the holy boldness that was released on the church in the book of Acts, (along with the amazing unity), we will not be able to fully accomplish God's purposes and may have a very difficult time even enduring to the end.

So, why are so few American Christians walking in the power of the Holy Spirit that was so evident in the early church? Is it because we have become the last day's Laodecian lukewarm church that thinks we are "rich and have need of nothing," and who feels so good about their material wealth that they don't recognize their true spiritual condition? At least to me it has become obvious after Y2K, 9/11 and other such warnings, that most Americans have become so confident in our military, economy and technology, that we don't really need God. We might put "God Bless America" on our signs during holidays or emergencies, but really we think we can handle it. And we're certainly not willing to make the changes in our hearts and lives or desperately cry out to God in ways that would allow Him to really move on our behalf.

There is also a whole segment of believers who have been taught and are convinced that we no longer need the gifts and power of the Holy Spirit since the Bible was published. But I wonder what they do with "the letter kills but the Spirit gives life"? Without the help of the Helper to enable us to fully understand the truth and then empower us to walk in it, the Word remains a mystery or brings condemnation. How little we know of God and His ways unless the Holy Spirit reveals them to us. And how futile and frustrating are our attempts to do the will of God without the power of the Spirit operating fully in our lives. Is it any wonder that so few believers are going on to maturity and growing up into or working out their salvation?

Many Christians who believe in the gifts and present day working of the Holy Spirit still do not understand the importance of releasing or being baptized in and continually filled with the Spirit of God. They understand that He is available but do not recognize the necessity to press into and learn how to daily walk with and work together with Him. Paul speaks of the need for every follower of Christ to walk in, be led by, controlled by, empowered by – literally, to live in the Spirit. It is meant to be a daily growing closer to and in unity with God as we surrender to and are progressively led by the Holy Spirit.

As we move into this time, which may well be the last of the last days, a close walk with the Lord is not an option, but it will be essential. To be in the place of the Psalm 91 protection we must be "under His wings" and "in the shadow of the Almighty," not following at a distance. If we are going to stay in step with the Lord, not lag behind or run ahead or turn aside, it will be necessary for us to train our ear to hear the still small voice of the Spirit.

The Bible speaks of a day when God will be gracious to His people in a time of judgment. Those who turn from their idols and false worship will experience His blessings and walk in divine guidance. When they begin to stray to the right or left, their ears will hear a voice behind them say "This is the way, walk in it." Sensitivity and obedience to the voice of the Spirit is crucial in the end times, which Jesus said would be characterized by great deception. Our enemy will be raging against the followers of Christ, and as the father of lies, he will be doing all he can to turn us away from the Lord and His purposes. Unless we have taken time to listen and have learned how to distinguish the voice of the Spirit in the midst of all the other voices clamoring for our attention, it will be very difficult to navigate the treacherous waters of the end times. No wonder the Lord warns that many will be deceived and fall away during this time preceding His return.

How then, do we learn to discern and follow the voice of the Holy Spirit in this very crucial hour? Much depends on both the quantity and quality of the time we spend with the Lord. In many ways it is just like my relationship with my wife (or any relationship that I want to grow deeper and be strong). If I rarely spend time with her, and when I am with her my mind is often on other things, how well do I really get to know her? On the other hand when I determine to make her a priority by being with her on a regular basis and really focusing on what she says and does, then our relationship will continue to grow. We have worked through many difficulties and misunderstandings through the years because of our willingness to make honest, open communication an essential part of our life together. Especially in the beginning of our relationship, we determined to set aside daily times to talk about our day or share things that interested or concerned us. Since we are both good communicators, talking was seldom a problem, but we did have to learn and really work on our listening skills. On a marriage enrichment weekend we learned how to really listen and reflect back to the other what we thought we heard without getting distracted by formulating our response after the first thing the person says. We were taught to listen to everything that was spoken and even ask questions to clarify and be certain we got the true meaning of what was spoken.

Wouldn't our relationship with God be much stronger if we followed these same principles? What if we set aside time everyday to talk with Him in prayer and then actually made an effort to hear what He wanted to tell us? The truth is that He has already spoken to us through His Word and though His Son but few people take time to really listen and seek to apprehend the full message. How many Christians see Jesus only as the one who provides forgiveness of sins, but they know little or nothing of salvation to the uttermost and of the sanctification that comes as we walk with Him and become conformed to His image?

And I can't help wondering how many Christians in American have thoroughly read and studied the entire Bible or if they have they even read it at all? My guess is that many never or rarely open the Word, which is collecting dust on the shelf, and that most have never read through the entire Bible let alone taken regular times to study and digest it.

Even those of us who have established a consistent time of daily devotions to pray and read the Word find it hard to fit God into our schedule the rest of the day. I am still trying to learn how to commune with the Lord every day by making an effort to talk with Him and really listen to what He has to say. It's so easy to just get busy making a plan and working our plan until we simply forget about the Lord much of the day (unless we run into trouble and need to ask for help). And if you're anything like me, even when I do take time to talk with Him or listen, my mind is running on all I need to do, so that it's almost impossible to hear what He wants to say.

The Lord still leads me in spite of my inability to stay attentive and focused, probably because I try to keep my heart right toward Him. Often I look back at my life and I am amazed to see His hand directing so much of what has taken place without me being aware of His guidance. But I would like to be more intentional about my walk with the Lord. My desire and my need is to daily be in constant and intimate fellowship with the Holy Spirit, to purposefully talk to and listen for His voice throughout my days with the determination to do whatever He says. That may well be the greatest need of every Christian as we prepare for the Lord's coming in these very exciting but perilous times.

35

The Fear of the Lord

I have been asking the Lord how to end this book and He reminded me of something He had told me recently. It was a time when we had been travelling all over the region doing corporate prayer and worship with pastors and intercessors. While there had been a number of small blessings from these meetings, we still felt we were a long way from the revival and great breakthrough that we desire and desperately need. After all our efforts to seek Him and usher in the last day's outpouring of the Spirit before the coming of the Lord, I knew there was something we were missing. So I asked God what was lacking, and His answer shocked me! I'm sure that was His intention for me and for His church so I will pass it along to you...

God clearly spoke to me that the thing we are lacking, which prevents Him from coming, is the Fear of the Lord. He said there is no fear of God in our nation or the world, and very little even in the church. Because of this, His delay is another sign of His love and mercy. He is giving us time to prepare our hearts knowing that His coming in all His glory will be judgment to those who are not ready even as it will be glorious for those who are. Thus, "the great and terrible Day of the Lord!"

He also reminded me that "the fear of the Lord is the beginning of wisdom." I remembered that truth from scripture but asked Him to further explain it to me. When you see God and reverence Him for who He is, you will also begin to see everything in your life from His perspective rather

Rom. 12: 1 & 2
Mal. 3:6
Heb. 13:8

than seeing Him and everything else from man's perspective. That is wisdom. It brings you to the place where you quickly and fully "present your whole self as a living sacrifice". In doing so you will "not be conformed to this world but transformed by the renewing of your mind so that you will prove (by obedience) that the will of God is not only acceptable but good and even perfect."

As I reflected on the fear of the Lord, I began to see how it had been lost in our society. One group has simply walked away from Him and no longer believes or loves Him nor obeys His Word. Another segment of the church, probably out of reaction to religious legalism that tries to get people in line and control them, has drifted to the opposite extreme of being too familiar and casual with His presence. Few have found the balance of cultivating an extravagant love while maintaining holy fear of the Lord. I'm learning that the two actually go together – you can't fully understand His love apart from His holiness and His holiness brings you to a deeper knowledge of His love.

At first it seemed like a contradiction to finish this writing with the fear of the Lord when I have already stated that it's all about love. What about the wayward woman who washed Jesus feet with her tears or Mary who sat at His feet and enjoyed His fellowship or John, the beloved disciple, who laid his head on Jesus' chest? How can these acts of love be reconciled with the Biblical admonition to fear the Lord?

Some have concluded that the God of the New Testament is different from the one of the Old, that He's a kinder, gentler God. Or they emphasize that we're now in the dispensation of grace as opposed to the law. But my Bible says God is "the same yesterday, today and forever" and that He never changes. Also, what about all those years God sent prophets to plead with His people to turn back to Him before He finally brought judgment? And what about Ananias and Saphira or the judgments of Revelation that will occur at the end of the age?

God also reminded me that when Jesus came to reveal the Father's heart by demonstrating His love He first laid aside the fullness of His glory in order to become a man. This enabled people to approach Him, to hear His words and receive His ministry, but most did not fully recognize who He was until after the resurrection. They looked at Jesus more as one of them, as a prophet and teacher, but mostly as the son of man rather than the Son of God. Even His disciples who had seen all the miracles and heard the teachings, including those who had been to the mount of

Transfiguration and Peter who had the revelation of the Christ, did not fully comprehend who Jesus was until He had risen from the dead.

I was also reminded that John, who called himself the beloved disciple and considered himself Jesus' best friend, had a very different reaction when He had a vision of the Lord's return in Revelation. The same one who had laid his head on Jesus' chest as they reclined at the table, an act of friendship and devotion, would also "fall on his face like a dead man" when he saw a vision of Jesus in all His glory. Since this is how Jesus will be when He comes again, we need to somehow cultivate an attitude of holy fear and respect along with a deep love and devotion.

I believe the Lord has given me some understanding of how these two – love and fear – can actually work together to bring us to the Lord and keep us close to Him, preparing us for His return. While the fear of the Lord (and hell!) can bring us to a decision for Christ, only a passionate love will motivate us to develop the relationship He desires and fulfill the purpose He has for us. And when the love grows cold, which happens in every relationship and will happen to many in the stress and trouble of the last days, then the fear of the Lord will hold us until we can stir up the faith and passion. Also, our deep love will keep us from staying at a distance from God out of fear, while our fear will keep us from being too familiar or casual with Him so that we compromise and presume upon His mercy and grace.

Like faith and works, the two are meant to compliment and perfect one another. A true and deep love will help us grow in respect and a holy fear, and at the same time, a holy fear will strengthen our love while keeping it in the proper perspective. To further explain how these work together and why we need both, the Lord reminded me of a great example in both the Old and New Testament.

The first example of a person who learned this balance between a holy fear and a passionate love was King David, who was declared to be a man after God's heart. Through all his years of worship and seeking the Lord, he had developed a great love and longing for the Presence of God. When he became king, he made it a priority to bring back the Ark of the Covenant, the presence of God to Jerusalem. However, he learned the hard way (the cost of a man's life) that good intentions are not enough.

David gained a healthy fear of the holiness of God and the realization that we cannot be hasty or casual in approaching Him. His passionate love made him determined to still bring in God's presence (even if he died in the process), but he was much more respectful and intentional on his second attempt, which pleased God and was successful.

In the New Testament the Apostle Paul had the same understanding of how fear and love of God can work together to prepare us to meet Him.

II Cor. 5:9
II Cor. 5:14 & 15
II Cor. 5: 10 & 11

Certainly Paul was one who made it clear through his words and actions that his main ambition, whether by life or death, was to please the Lord. He also shows in the verses that follow that his motivation was fueled by both a compelling love and a holy fear.

While the love of Christ (both Paul's love for Jesus and His love for Paul, profoundly revealed through the cross) is what controls, constrains and compels Paul to live only for the Lord, he never loses track of the reality that we all must stand before Him one day to give an account. When our love for God is not as strong as it once was and our motivation to obey and serve Him wanes, the thought of appearing before the judgment seat of Christ to reveal what we have done with what we've been given, can be a powerful force. For Paul, and for all Christians, the fear of God is not so much of judgment or loss of rewards, but of falling short of the grace we've been given and doing far less than we could have to honor and glorify the One who gave His all for us.

As we long for and prepare ourselves for the return of our Beloved Lord, let us seek to develop a holy fear and respect of who He is while continuing to stir up a deep love and passion for Him. The one will help get us ready even as the other will press us into His presence. And who knows how much time remains before we stand before Him and live with Him forever...

36

What Manner of Persons Ought We to Be?!!

As I come to the end of this writing, I am considering what Jesus Himself would say to us and has said to us regarding His return. Since the Day of the Lord will come as a thief in the night – sudden and unexpected – He warns us to Watch, Pray and Be Ready! Knowing our lack of discernment and diligence, He also provides many signs that will point to His coming and the preparations we should make for that awesome day. The Bible is full of end time's prophecies that, with the help of the Holy Spirit, can tell us of the things to come and may soon take place.

It doesn't take a Bible scholar to recognize that the world is rapidly moving toward a time of crisis and drastic change – you only have to watch the news. While it may be dangerous to try to fit everything into the prophetic puzzle, some things are pretty obvious and the picture is truly beginning to unfold. We dare not continue on with business as usual, ignoring the Word, the signs around us, and the voices of the prophets. They are all together pointing toward and loudly declaring the soon return of our Lord and Savior Jesus Christ.

II Pet. 3:11
II Pet. 3:14
I Jn. 5:16-18
Heb. 12:10,11

I know it's difficult for our minds to comprehend and our heart to believe that this is indeed the time. We must shake ourselves out of our slumber, apprehension, and our unbelief. The organ prelude has begun, everything is coming into place for the wedding to start, but has the Bride made herself ready? Are we ready for the refining fires of tribulation that will precede and prepare us for His coming?

In light of all these things it is time for the true church of Jesus Christ to arise and shine as God's glory arises upon the earth preceding His return. First, however, we must sincerely ask ourselves some very important questions and be ready to make whatever changes are necessary when we have the answers.

Peter asks two very poignant questions regarding the Day of the Lord's return and even provides suggestions for the answer. The first one is very simple: "what manner of persons ought we to be?" or "how now shall we live?" This brings us back to "who is the Lord returning for?" and "what kind of bride does the Lord desire, deserve and demand?" Peter goes on to say "in holy conduct and godliness looking for and hastening the coming of the day of God," indicating that our preparation can actually speed up and bring about His return. That shouldn't surprise us since every wedding begins pretty much when the bride is ready.

The second question is implied and even more personal and challenging: how do you want to be found by Him? When the Lord arrives, will you feel great joy and excitement or will it be more like worry and dread? Will your first words be "Praise God!" or "Oh, no!" Much depends on the condition of your heart and the depth of your relationship with Jesus at that time, whether you can come to Him in confidence or your own heart condemns you because you have not abided in and been perfected by love.

When we stand before Jesus, the question will not be "Did you follow all the rules?" or "Did you clean up your act?" or even "Did you do your job?" The only thing that will matter is : "Did you learn to love?" It really does all come down to loving God and loving others. If we will stir up a holy passion for the Lord, then the purity, power and productivity will naturally follow. Without love all of our best efforts will gain nothing eternal (though it may bring immediate, worldly acclamation and gratification), and even worse, it could cause us to be ones who hear, "Depart form me. I never knew you!"

Everyone who calls himself a Christian must begin to carefully examine his own heart to see if he is truly in the faith. Have I fully opened my heart to receive God's amazing love? Have I wholly given myself to love Him, revealed by surrender and a wholehearted commitment to worship, serve and obey Him? Is He still the priority of my life, far more than anything or anyone else, or have I allowed other people or things to steal my affections so that my love for God has grown cold? It is time for us to be brutally honest about our true spiritual condition lest we, like the Laodecean church think we're rich and have need of nothing not realizing how far away from God and His purposes we are.

So many who claim to be Christian in America have become so casual and compromised in their faith that they are lukewarm at best. In fact, that level or style of Christianity is so prevalent in our nation that someone who is truly passionate for the Lord is considered a fanatic and accused of being in a cult. We are convinced that the little bit we give to God is good enough and that He would be pleased that we give Him anything at all. However, Jesus makes it clear that this kind of Christianity makes God sick and in truth it is not at all what it means to be a follower of Christ. God would rather have us be cold and not even claim to be a Christian than to say we are a believer and live like the world which is nothing but a negative witness.

Of course the Lord's desire and demand for all of His people is that we are passionately in love with Him, and we need to reveal that love through our wholehearted worship, obedience and service. To the lukewarm church Jesus said to "repent and be zealous" by seeking Him and all that He desires to give His people rather than the things of this world. In order to bring us back to Him and show His deep love for us, the Lord promises to rebuke and chasten those who have drifted away. Those who trust in His love and submit to His discipline will be "partakers of His holiness' and receive the "peaceable fruit of righteousness". Do not despise the discipline of the Lord but rather surrender to Him and trust that He is preparing you for His coming and all He desires to do in and through you before He returns.

It has been sad and even frustrating for me (and I'm sure it is for God) to see how far this nation, which was largely founded by Christians on Biblical principles, continues its downward slide. We have fallen so far away from our foundation that even our president has stated that America is no longer a Christian nation. More and more people are leaving or straying away from the church and many who still attend have only a form of religion but are denying the power of a loving relationship with the loving God. Even those of us who once had a very close walk with and passion for the Lord have settled into our busy routines while neglecting the better part.

Truly, God is calling us back to our first love. It seems like every book I've picked up or has been recommended or given to me lately has focused on love – understanding and receiving God's amazing love for us and responding with a wholehearted love for Him. This is not a time to be drifting away or neglecting so great a salvation by allowing out love for the Lord to grow cold or even lukewarm. We must do all we can to stir up a holy fire or passion for our coming King and Bridegroom. Instead of the compromise and indifference so evident in the American church today, Jesus is coming for those who are looking and longing for Him and are diligently preparing for His return and the wedding celebration.

Getting back to our first love, the love we had for Jesus when we initially opened our heart to Him as Lord and Savior, is a matter or priority. Like Mary, we must choose the better part, the one thing that is necessary, which is to spend quality time with the Lord and listen to what He is saying to us and His church at this crucial hour. As we enjoy and become confident in His love, it will enable us to trust and endure whatever may be coming upon this world or in our lives before He returns. Those who endure to the end will be saved and purified for His coming.

At the same time, fully receiving and living in His love will stir in us a holy passion to be fully prepared for His soon return. We will diligently cooperate with the Holy Spirit to be a beautiful bride – without spot, wrinkle or blemish. As we allow and assist the Spirit with the work that needs to be done in us, we will also be preparing for all God desires to do through us before His glorious appearing. While great darkness will cover the earth as Satan works through the forces of the anti-Christ, the glory of God will arise upon His people. The last day's church will be led and empowered by the Spirit to forcefully advance the Kingdom and gather the great harvest of souls at the end of the age.

There is so much more I could share that the Lord has showed me in His Word and through my walk with Him these 30 years, but I've already written more than I intended when I started months ago. Just as one chapter has led to another, perhaps one writing will lead to the next, as the Lord directs and time permits.

Let me close by saying it is not my intention to write a "how to" book on preparing the bride that would provide everyone with specific step-by-step program to get ready. My main purpose has been to loudly shout a wake-up call to those who are sleeping that the Day may be coming much sooner than we realize. I have also attempted to share a general outline of the kind of people the Lord will be looking for when He returns as well as some things we can do to prepare ourselves for Him. As you draw close to Him to seek His face and hear His voice, Jesus will fill in the specific details for you.

In the world every wedding is different based on the desires and preparation of the bride, but in the great wedding to come our desire will be to please our Bridegroom King. With that in mind we could benefit from the book of Esther. In order to find favor and be selected she submitted to those in authority over her (Uncle Mordecai) and the king's servant (symbolic of the Holy Spirit) through the entire preparation process rather than devising her own good plan. As a result, she not only won the King's favor but put herself in a place to save many of her people during a very turbulent time in their history.

In these perilous times of the last day may you also find favor with the King as you open your heart to fully receive His love. And may your love for Him overflow in worship and obedience as you trust and surrender to Him and His work in and through your life in this very crucial and exciting hour. I hope that these words have helped you in some way. Thank-you for sharing this journey with me .

In His love and for His glory.

Jim Cousineau, a bondservant of Jesus Christ

Lord Jesus, we cry out for mercy for us, your people, and for this nation. We pray "even in judgement remember mercy" (Hab3:2) and "spare your people, Oh Lord." (Joel 2:17) Turn our hearts wholly to You that we may love and serve You alone in sincerity and truth. Fill us with a holy fear and passion that we may live only to please you and glorify your name. Help us, Lord, to be the beautiful, faithful bride that you are desiring and for whom you will soon return to receive yourself. Holy Spirit, we implore you to take control of every area of our lives. Give us wisdom and grace to be more like Jesus and do everything He asks us to do in these exciting and perilous times. Whether by life or death may you be glorified in me and in your church forever. We love you, Jesus, and lay our lives before you. Prepare us fully for your coming and use us in whatever ways you desire for your kingdom and your glory. Amen!